A RUM OLE NORFOLK YEAR

Further details of Poppyland Publishing titles can be found at
www.poppyland.co.uk
*where clicking on the 'Support and Resources' button
will lead to pages specially compiled to support this book*

Join us for more Norfolk and Suffolk stories and background at
www.facebook.com/poppylandpublishing
and follow **@poppylandpub**

KEITH SKIPPER'S
A Rum Ole Norfolk Year

POPPYLAND
PUBLISHING

First published 2016 by Poppyland Publishing, Cromer, NR27 9AN
www.poppyland.co.uk
ISBN 978 1 909796 30 0
Designed and typeset in 12 on 14.4 pt Gilgamesh
Printed by Lightning Source

Picture credits:

Author's collection Both covers, 9, 10, 16, 24, 29, 35, 46, 48, 52, 57, 71, 76, 80, 84, 91, 94, 100, 103
Paul Damen 20
Poppyland Publishing 14, 15, 37, 40, 60, 64, 67, 96

Other titles by Keith Skipper from Poppyland Publishing:

Norfolk in a Nutshell, where Keith muses on what makes Norfolk a bit different.
Keith Skipper's Norfolk Scrapbook, a treasure trove where Keith looks back over his life in the
    media.

DEDICATION

Dedicated to all our wonderful Norfolk wordsmiths who keep building on the basics handed down by mentors with time, patience and vision.

"It has long been an axiom of mine that the little things are infinitely the most important" — Arthur Conan Doyle

ACKNOWLEDGEMENTS

I am grateful to countless readers, listeners and homely enthusiasts who have kept me amply supplied with small but beautifully formed bits and pieces throughout a long and rewarding Norfolk career as scribe, broadcaster and entertainer.

Special salutes for the Eastern Daily Press and associated weekly newspapers for staying true to the "little things are important" mantra and so allowing me to include rich examples in this selection devoted to a host of special people operating in a special place.

Warmest thanks to Peter Stibbons at Poppyland Publishing for backing yet another local adventure with his customary expertise and enthusiasm. And a posy of praise for my wife Diane, who remains steadfastly in favour of the old saying that behind every scatterbrain writer there lurks a sound and sensible organising figure.

INTRODUCTION

One of my first jobs as a raw cub reporter dispatched to the mean streets of Thetford in the mellow autumn sunshine of 1962 involved meeting, mardling, connecting and collecting.

I knocked on doors and introduced myself to a wide range of local "movers and shakers" as the town squared up to the challenges of London overspill. My role as a nosey interloper from mid-Norfolk could have been dismissed as some sort of quirky afterthought.

My general reception, however, was cordial and welcoming, boosted perhaps by enthusiastic offers of regular publicity in the local press. Thin lines between that precious commodity and campaigns touting personal aggrandisement, blatantly free advertising and galloping hobby-horses could wait until I'd got hold of the basics.

Several of Thetford's finest on my initial list became valuable contacts during a short but career-shaping stint among them, church ministers leading the way. The Rev Len Hodson (Methodist), Pastor Moore (Baptist) and the Rev Rachael Storr (Congregational) gave me every chance to sample a blossoming ecumenical spirit.

They helped provide a healthy crop of "town paragraphs" every week. The fact I can remember their names and see their faces well over half-a-century later indicates how well our arrangements went, especially as they occasionally pointed me towards good stories featuring members of their congregations.

I took this affection and respect for what my older colleagues called bread-and-butter items into the rest of my full-time newspaper career and onto the airwaves when it counted during parochially-spiced years with BBC Radio Norfolk. Daily programmes were all the better for the what's-on diary, chemists' rota and listeners' limericks featuring village names and letters with attitude from proud indigenous remnants.

When I started to keep a comprehensive daily diary just as 1984 dawned, I knew there must be room for smaller local items to spice up my pages and underline Norfolk's well-deserved reputation for dewin' diffrunt and then confusing the rest of the world even more by laughing at the results.

The general idea behind this book, my 40th off the Norfolk production line, is to salute the downright silly, acknowledge the outstanding achievers, bless those able to brighten the bleakest of days and congratulate all with a penchant for attracting publicity in the name of home-grown posterity.

There are a few recurring themes — such as loyal service to local communities and the changing face of country life — but these month-by-month selections from over 30 years of eavesdropping and jotting around my native patch tend to emphasise a natural passion for the mildly unbecoming or markedly unusual.

For example, the following pages reveal what were called "hideosities" by a local councillor, who had a pacemaker fitted at the age of 107, where it was planned to put horses into nappies, why a bride turned up for her wedding in a wheelbarrow and when Sherba, Lady Baa Baa and Ewesain Bolt caused a village flutter.

It's been hard graft but richly rewarding in the search for notable nuggets among thousands of pages devoted to my daily doings and observations. Thank goodness what started as a gentle habit has become a proud obsession.

It just goes to show how respect for those bread-and-butter items can lead to a tantalising spread of fancy cakes, iced buns and a tasty roll-call of savoury Norfolk snippits.

KEITH SKIPPER
Cromer, 2016

Keith (right) with his first three EDP mentors — from the left, Charles Sharp of the Dereham office, John Kitson and Jim Wilson of the Thetford office.

JANUARY

BEYOND THE PAIL (1984) — With the new year hardly out of its cradle, a stirring literary breakthrough to celebrate. I spy the headline "Breckland to scrap honeycart" on the back page of the Eastern Daily Press. This must be the first time such a description has been pinned on the old night-soil wagon in our local paper in a serious report. Over 100 homes in Breckland still use pail closets. They're given five years to scrap them. The district council is to drop its collection service in 1989, leaving households five years to make alternative arrangements.

Wally Feeke and the Litcham honeycart.

MALLARDY SPLASH (1985) — Bramerton Woods End pub landlord Peter Tallowin is drying out after his New Year stunt along the River Yare. He takes to his water-skis dressed as a giant mallard. His antics have blossomed since he was thrown into the river 11 years ago on January 1st. Since then he's raised money for charity with fancy dress ski-ing on the first day of the year. He's fortified with hot rum punch this time but does not have the benefit of a wet-suit.

TORKIN' PROPER (1987) — Hackles rise as I pick up the Eastern Daily Press and read a front page story featuring so-called education experts. They claim Norfolk children are seen — but not heard properly. So they're starting a project to teach the art of correct conversation. How can you teach conversation? Surely it's a spontaneous form of communication. I suspect this is another move towards dull uniformity, probably inspired by outsiders who neither understand nor appreciate the beauties of our dialect. It also adds fuel to the old suggestion that a rustic accent is a clear symptom of being thick.

STEPHEN STUCK (1987) — Embarrassed Stephen Burton spends an hour stuck in a baby swing on Bradwell playing field before firemen release him. His friend's mum smothers the 12-year-old with margarine but he remains stuck fast. Eventually, with a growing audience looking on, Gorleston firemen release the bolts at the bottom of the swing to allow Stephen to slide free. His mum comments: "This is the first time he's been away from his computer and out to play all holiday. It's probably ruined his trousers."

SWIFT VERDICT (1988) — A judge comes under immediate fire from leading figures in the town for likening King's Lynn to the salt mines of Siberia while addressing the jury during a Crown Court hearing. Judge Frederick Beezley, the Cambridge resident judge, makes his comment while explaining to the jury why he is adjourning the hearing earlier than usual. It is "unavoidable" that he has to attend a magistrates' meeting in Cambridge; "King's Lynn is not my normal county, and it is rather like being sent to the salt mines of Siberia".

REAL FALL GUY (1988) — Panto villain Roy Goodwin comes to a sticky end — for real. The farmer falls badly in a staged dive during a performance of Mother Goose at Harleston. He has a nasty gash under his chin. Three stitches are inserted between scenes to ensure the show can go on. Roy is fit to take his place for the final fling. A game trouper!

END OF COYPU (1989) — After eight years of intensive trapping the campaign to wipe out the coypu is declared an official success. The 240-strong team of trappers will each receive a termination bonus for getting rid of the South American rodents, introduced into East Anglia in the late 1920s. The original population of 3,000 expanded rapidly to an estimate 200,000 by the 1950s.

BE CAREFUL ... (1990) — Classic entry for the "I told you so!" Norfolk file. Plans to build a garage complex on Cromer's Holt Road are given the go-ahead. North Norfolk District Council had been opposed to further development in an Area of Outstanding Natural Beauty when the plan was first put forward last July. Now they admit defeat because they have already given themselves planning permission to build new council offices on a large slice of the land nearby.

CREEPING SUBURBS (1991) — An organic farmer, criticised by his parish council for spreading blood on his field, calls for more give-and-take in his community. Martin Green of Costessey says: "My family have worked this farm since 1923. The problem is that the suburbs have crept up on us and now we are surrounded by city dwellers. Many of them seem to have a Beatrix Potter view of the country". He adds a lot of people use the farmland as a public park and crops have been damaged by dogs and motor cycles.

CURTAIN CALL (1991) — A set of curtains covering the Lord Mayor's balcony window in Norwich City Hall are to be replaced. They are thought to have been there since the 1930s.

GRIN AND BARE IT (1992) — A group of local naturists are urged to fight for the right to continue using a Norfolk beach. They have been ordered to cover up on the beach at Waxham, a favourite haunt since the 1920s, because of a complaint of exhibitionism. The Central Council for British Naturism is persisting in efforts to persuade councillors to lift the ban.

TOURIST TRAFFIC (1993) — The RAC warns that urgent action is need to stop stretches of beautiful Norfolk grinding to a halt under the strain of tourist traffic. The motoring organisation rules out the prospect of a ban on cars in popular tourist haunts like the Broads — at least for the time being. But it warns in its "Cars in the Countryside" report that action must be taken in a region where a single slow-moving caravan can cause chaos on narrow roads.

DEN DISCOVERY (1994) — Four Attleborough youngsters can hardly believe their eyes when they stumble across a box filled with jewellery while making a den. It's been hidden in a peat sack and covered with leaves by a burglar who broke into homes on the town's Springfield estate three weeks ago. Delighted owner Hilary Hunter gives each of the lads a £5 reward. "It does restore your faith in young people" she says.

WINTER LIFT (1995) — I'm impressed by an article on Cromer in the Sunday Times. It's not one of those snide summaries by some clever metropolitan but a lyrical tribute from Richard Girling: "Few places on earth can seem more empty of promise than the English seaside on a rainy day in July. Few places can offer more buoyancy to the spirit than the same place on a sunny day in winter ..." He leaves with a cassette of songs recorded by Cromer Smugglers — "their tuneful melancholy caught our mood."

MINE'S A MUNCH! (1996) — Norfolk Wildlife Trust's "flying flock" are drafted in to restore a priceless piece of British history, the 4,000-year-old flint mines at Grimes Graves, near Brandon. The sheep, who normally munch their way around less prestigious sites, will spend the next three months grazing the overgrown Neolithic landscape to help promote the growth of wild flowers.

FAMILY DOUBLE (1998) — When people in North Creake need a helping hand, one man is always willing to pitch in. John Couzens gives up time to help the elderly and disabled who cannot tend their gardens and also helps raise money for good causes. Now the efforts of the 69-year-old retired agricultural worker bring him the title of North Creake Parishioner of the Year. It completes a family double. His sister, Ann Owen, collected the title 12 months ago for her contribution to village life, especially with help at the parish church.

BARBARA STARS (1999) — When Barbara Rix drops in on the count at a parish council by-election she expects to be a mere spectator. But she finishes with a starring role — by flipping a coin to decide the winner. She's the only member of the public to turn up for the count after residents at Surlingham, near Norwich, go to the polls to decide the council vacancy. A total of 110 votes are cast, 55 each for candidates Phyllis Gladwell and Anne Pinder. Protocol usually decides the winner by cutting a deck of cards. The returning officer doesn't have one and neither candidate is present. A 2p coin is produced and Barbara is asked to perform the vital flip. The toss favours Phyllis Gladwell.

NOT AGAIN! (2000) — Here we go again! I am asked for my views about a lifestyle survey claiming people in East Anglia are the happiest and most stress-free in the country. I must get busy with my "Norfolk is the worst for …" survey in a bid to stop all this flattering nonsense!

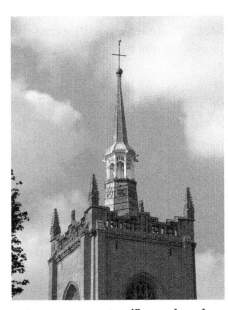

Controversy at Swaffham when the vicar is accused of turning off the chimes from the tower — but the situation is clarified around the need for accuarcy!

CLOCKING OUT (2001) — The chimes they are a'changing in Swaffham — and the vicar is about to get a ticking-off. Town councillors claim the Rev John Smith turned off the chimes at his church because the noise disrupted services. But the vicar says: "It's nonsense. I turned the chimes off because they were striking a quarter-of-an-hour fast.

COMFORTING ECHOES (2002) — Countryside around Aylsham looks stark and yet strangely attractive. We pass a shrouded Blickling Hall and stop for lunchtime sandwiches at one of our favourite spots on the outskirts of Itteringham. We call at the village shop run by the community and hear locals called by their first names, an echo of old village ways. An old man raises his stick in greeting as we pass through Erpingham and I warm myself on another comforting country image from the past.

SUCH IRONY! (2003) — What about this for supreme irony — or even infernal cheek? Wealthy weekend cottage owners in our area are being asked to rent out their rooms to local families in a bid to ease an affordable housing crisis. This pioneering move will see council officials advertise in London, ironically targeting people being blamed for fuelling the original problem! About 5,000 holiday homes across north Norfolk are owned by well-heeled outsiders, adding to the woes of true locals who cannot find or afford anywhere suitable to live.

SPITTING IMAGE (2004) — Spitting in the streets is such a problem in Thetford that local councillors are considering bringing back a Victorian by-law to ban it. They blame footballers' behaviour on the pitch for a resurgence of the disgusting habit. Antics of the stars are apparently being copied by people attempting to look cool. Of course, there's a serious concern police won't be able to enforce any law — same argument is doing the rounds about mobile phones being used at the driving wheel — but it must be good for this nasty spitting business to attract such attention.

NELSON TOUCH (2005) — People entering the county will now be reminded of Norfolk's favourite son, thanks to 28 road signs saluting Horatio Nelson. The signs, stating "Norfolk — Nelson's County", and depicting the county shield, have been made possible thanks to a donation from turkey tycoon and Nelson admirer Bernard Matthews. He unveils the first sign on the Norfolk-Suffolk border at Scole, near Diss.

Whichever road you arrive in Norfolk by, you'll be reminded of one of her favourite sons, thanks to Bernard Matthews.

Norfolk champion of traditional baking Norman Olley eventually admitted he could no longer compete with the big supermarkets.

MAST MILESTONE (2006) — The Tacolneston television mast, one of Norfolk's best-known landmarks, is celebrating its 50th birthday. The 505ft structure became the main BBC transmitter for viewers in East Anglia in 1956, replacing a temporary 20ft aerial. It heralded a new era, not only for TV users, but radio listeners as well.

TOO CROWDED (2007) — It was 40 years ago when pop star Jimi Hendrix performed at a packed Orford Cellar in Norwich. I went along with the local press corps — but left soon after the start because I couldn't see anything and it was too hot and crowded. I retired to a quiet pub nearby for a pint of shandy and packet of crisps. Hendrix fans called me "barmy" for missing such a musical treat.

LAW AND ORDER (2008) — Excerpt from community news, Worstead section, in North Norfolk News: "Law and order: PCSO Wibberley reported the theft and recovery of one bike. There had also been one domestic incident, noise in the shelter, one incident of egg-throwing, rubbish being put on cars and mooning." Den of iniquity!

CHAMPION QUITS (2010) — He's been Norfolk's champion of traditionally-baked bread for nearly 40 years, his 102-year-old independent bakery serving schools, businesses and thousands of people with their daily loaves. Now Norman Olley, 66, is calling it a day in the fight against the insurmountable tide of cheap bread from supermarkets. He's closed his shop in Dereham and his stall on Norwich Market and is baking his last loaf in his traditional oven at North Elmham Bakery. Norman laments: "Soon there'll be no quality bakers left to compete with the supermarkets. We will be forgotten."

PIER PEACE (2011) — I have Cromer Pier to myself in late afternoon as two lads on bikes scurry from behind the theatre and folk in the box office call it a day. The peace is so welcome on my first call of the new year. Easy to go slow, ponder the future, savour the past and watch the gulls swoop. This truly deserve a place in any "Wonders of Norfolk" department.

CLEY FLUTTER (2012) — What a flutter on New Year's Day! Hundreds of bird-watchers land at Cley Marshes nature reserve for a glimpse of the western sandpiper, which has made this location its winter home for five weeks. Enthusiasts make special trips from as far away as Norway and Germany to see the North American wader, never before seen in Norfolk — and spotted only eight times in the United Kingdom.

PAGET TRIBUTE (2014) — Descendants of Sir James Paget join the congregation at Great Yarmouth Minister for a special service to mark the 200th anniversary of the pioneering surgeon's birth. Civic leaders from across the region and staff from the hospital in Gorleston named after him join in tributes to one of the borough's most famous sons.

SHANNOCK SHOOTERS (2015) — An afternoon out — in Sheringham! Yes, a brief sortie over the border for lunch and mooching. David Starling, in his 80s but still active in the family shop, says he continues to rise at 5.30am to oversee newspaper rounds. His son recalls a slice of local rivalry in the 1960s when the Shannocks visited the Crabs for a football derby. The visiting spectators were armed with pea-shooters and aimed constantly at the Cromer goalkeeper.

EARLY BIRD (2016) — A strange alarm call gets me out of bed earlier than usual. I pull back the curtains to spy a pheasant on the fence below. A plaintive cry comes across as a sort of strangled chortle. The bird peers at me, wobbles in the wind and then flies onto the roof for a short-lived impression of a weather vane. It must have been blown off its usual course. Colourful start to the day.

FEBRUARY

SLICES OF HISTORY (1985) — Youngsters at a Norfolk village school tuck into their own slices of history. Pupils at Flegg Primary School enjoy their annual supply of penny loaves. The custom dates back to 1527. Originally the bread was handed out to poor children of the parish but now all have an equal chance to share in the tradition. Loaves are bought from rent received for a half-acre field opposite the school which a mystery benefactor left for that purpose over four centuries ago. The land has become known as Penny Loaf Field. It was called Halfpenny Loaf Field until inflation caught up with it.

NAUGHTY JIM (1986) — Norfolk County Football Association chairman Jim Chandler is left red-faced with embarrassment during Downham Youth's 5-4 win over Acle in their John Savage Cup semi-final, Poor old Jim earns a ticking-off from the referee minutes after the match has started — because his umbrella clashes with Downham's yellow strip!

SHOW—STEALER (1987) — Sherry the Shetland pony steals the show at the Theatre Royal pantomime service in St Peter Mancroft Church in Norwich. According to the programme, Sherry is down to make a "contribution" while Michelle Summers reads a farmyard tale. Perhaps Sherry misunderstands "contribution" because with back to audience she answers a call of nature which encourages the vicar, Canon David Sharp, to call for bucket and spade.

FRESH ROLE (1987) — A signal box made redundant through electrification of the railway line at Swainsthorpe finds a new home beside the sea at Wells. The box, as tall as a house, is transported 40 miles by road on a low loader to become the centrepiece of the Wells and Walsingham Light Railway.

BONUS BELOW (1989) — A luxury £200,000 penthouse, thought to be the most expensive flat in Norwich, is sold with the added bonus of its own novel burglar alarm. The police station is downstairs. The apartment is one of a dozen on the top floor of Dencora House in Theatre Street.

PLAYING ON (1991) — An organist who has been delighting church congregations for over 55 years says she has no intention of giving up. "I'm going to play for as long as I can" vows 72-year-old Phyllis Warner of Shipdham. She has played in 22 parishes — and that's a record to take some beating.

WORTHY TRIBUTE (1991) - A good ole Norfolk boy is the subject of "This Is Your Life" on national television. Veteran Caister lifeboatman Skipper Woodhouse takes it all in his stride. The story of the 79-year-old's eventful life unfolds before 12 million viewers. He sits relaxed, wearing his fisherman's jacket and cap in front of the cameras. Host Michael Aspel is charmed by a character whose Norfolk dialect is "from another time and another place." Worthy tribute to a grand local lad.

"Skipper" Jack Woodhouse of Caister. As well as being the subject of "This is Your Life", he left Terry Wogan lost for words when a guest on his television show.

THINKING TWICE (1992) – Poor prospects on the land are discouraging a new generation from a career in agriculture, according to Norfolk National Farmers' Union chairman John Place. Young people are no longer automatically expected to follow in father's footsteps. "I would probably think twice about encouraging my family to start a career in farming today" says Mr Place, who farms at Tunstead. A survey of more than 25,000 farms says one in three farmers has no successor.

HAMMER BLOW (1993) – Half-a-century after having his knuckles rapped by a strict schoolmistress for being naughty, estate agent John Dewing is in charge of selling off his former village school at Bradenham. It closed last summer. It's a mixed blessing for John, who welcomes the business but is sad to be signalling the end of an era. "It gave me a good grounding. There were two mistresses there in those days and they stood no nonsense. I had my knuckles rapped with a ruler every now and again."

END OF ROUND (1993) – Mileham baker Frank Minister is being forced to close his family-run business because he can't afford to modernise the traditional bakery. New European Community regulations spell the end for the family, baking bread for local villagers for more than half-a-century. Edna Walpole, a customer for most of those years, says: "I am very sad about it. It's a real shame and we'll all miss him."

BECK AND CALL? (1994) – Gordon Beck of Lingwood has walked about 20 miles a day, seven days a week, on the Reedham marshes since he became a marshman 23 years ago. Now he's to swap the rigours of this outdoor life for the comfort of his armchair as he retires – and hands over the job to his nephew, Jim Beck.

BEATING BLIZZARD (1996) – Actress Nyree Dawn Porter, at the Theatre Royal this week in the musical version of Great Expectations, will long remember her trip to Norwich. Her journey by road from Birmingham takes her into the heart of the Great Blizzard. She arrives after about 19 hours, about as long as her character, Miss Havisham, would have taken to do the journey in a Victorian stagecoach. Miss Porter spends the night in an AA relay rescue vehicle. But the show goes on!

JOURNEY'S END (1997) – Kenneth Groom calls it a day after 76 years behind the wheel of an assortment of cars on Norfolk's roads. Kenneth, a 92-year-old retired medical welfare officer from Hellesdon, bought his first car in 1922. "It started with a handle on the front. I don't feel safe anymore with all these modern mad hatters."

DREAM DOUBLE (1999) – Two Norfolk octogenarians achieve every golfer's dream – a hole-in-one. George Goram, 81, is first when he drives from the 115-yard par three 17th at Royal Cromer Golf Club. While he basks in the afterglow, Jack Hysom, 82, is preparing to pitch in with his own one-stroke wonder at the same hole.

HOME WINS (2000) – Residents of two Norfolk parishes celebrate victory in a battle to keep their homes out of Thetford. The town council is thwarted in its bid to swallow up three roads in the parishes of Croxton and Brettenham as Breckland Council cabinet members refuse to back the boundary changes. Villagers who live on Hill House Lane and Heathlands in Croxton and Arlington Way in Brettenham fought a big campaign against change which would have boosted town council coffers to the tune of £7,000 in council tax.

SEA CHANGES (2001) – Our seaside towns must look to the bright lights of Las Vegas for inspiration! Sea Changes, published by the English Tourism Council, is heralded as a blueprint for rejuvenation of Britain's bucket-and-spade resorts. Traditional destinations like Yarmouth, Cromer, Sheringham, Hunstanton and Lowestoft must adopt a "fresh vision" and a "masterplan for action" if they are to compete with the more-chic holiday spots. I say leave well alone!

PORCH SERVICE (2002) – A Norfolk vicar and his congregation hold their morning service in the church porch after the door is jammed shut in an attempted burglary. The Rev Alan Greenhough and about 15 members of his flock crowd into the porch of All Saints' Church at Stibbard.

PAYING BACK (2003) — This makes sound sense ... a Norfolk church hit by an arson attack has been tidied up by the youngsters who caused the damage. The four boys and a girl were caught on CCTV cameras setting light to the altar at Diss Parish Church. They were interviewed by police and then referred to the county's Youth Offending Team instead of going through the court system. Only one of the children had been in trouble with the police before and all agreed to do two hours of reparation work to pay back to the community for their misdemeanours.

ROYAL FLAVOUR (2005) — We're told the Queen can do a good Norfolk accent. Princess Michael of Kent says our monarch features our local vernacular in her favourite party pieces. Good to have a royal seal of approval for our efforts to keep something precious alive. I'm asked for my views by the local press and radio stations. I suggest it might be helpful if the Queen has a mardle with the BBC and ITV before the next production purporting to be set in Norfolk.

LIKELY STORIES (2006) — A frozen squirrel falling from a tree, a wasp crawling up a trouser leg and a flying kebab — these are among bizarre reasons given by people making claims for damage to their vehicle. The unusual stories are among those detailed by insurance giant Norwich Union as it makes public some of the weirdest claims it has received.

TABLES TURNED (2007) — They are the men and women usually tasked with making sure events at the top tables run smoothly. But this weekend sees the tables turned for toastmasters across the country as they gather at Park Farm Hotel in Hethersett for their annual meeting.

THAT'S OPTIMISM! (2008) — Uplifting little incident worth noting after perambulations on Cromer Pier. A local veteran sitting in one of the shelters calls me over for a word. "I'll be 90 in three years' time!" he exclaims proudly. I tell him I love that kind of optimism.

LORD'S MILESTONE (2009) — Grand gathering at Sheringham Little Theatre to salute Lord Robin Walpole on his 70th birthday. He

Former Sheringham lifeboat coxswain Brian Pegg was also a Salvation Army stalwart. He played football for both Sheringham and Cromer — and lived to tell the tale.

reached the milestone in December but it was deemed too difficult to get folk together for the specific date. Family and friends out in force today. I'm invited to appear on the entertainment bill. I compose a few lines in Norfolk dialect, attributing the effort to local character Horry Pightle.

RETURN TICKET (2010) — Almost 51 years ago, 16-year-old Janet Hardwick bought the last ticket for the train travelling into Whitwell and Reepham station before it was closed for good in a nationwide purge. Now she's able to travel on the line again to join celebrations to mark the first anniversary of its restoration.

TASTY INSULTS! (2011) — Sunday Times restaurant reviewer A.A. Gill upsets Norfolk after a visit to the Rose and Crown at Snettisham. His tasty insults include "If Norfolk didn't exist, we would have to make it up and then regret it" and "Norfolk is a backward place to allocate dark lusts, incest and idiocy." He sums up the county as "The hernia on the end of England." Such dazzling wit deserves a free meal and honorary citizenship.

NO ADVERTISING! (2012) — Screen star John Hurt, who has lived just along the coast from Cromer for three years, says of Norfolk in an Eastern Daily Press interview: "It's a wonderfully empty county. I like the space, which is difficult to find in this country." Well, if you like the space so much, Mr Hurt, keep quiet and stop advertising it! Same goes for other celebrities who have taken a shine to our county, John Major, Martin Shaw and Amanda Holden among them. I'm scared of the way "star" endorsements simply attract too many others, the vast majority worthy of membership of the bland "bolt-hole brigade."

"A NICE BLOKE" (2013) — Former Sheringham lifeboat coxswain Brian Pegg dies at 81. A Salvation Army stalwart and talented musician, he got on well with his Cromer counterparts. Hardly surprising when you learn he played football for both towns — and lived to tell the tale! He drank lemonade while other members of the crew made merry — but never looked for a halo to float above his sou'wester. " I'm not a bible-thumper but I know the rules" he said as locals and strangers alike queued up to hear his banter, gentle and amusing without a hint of spite. Perhaps a Cromer resident pays the perfect tribute: "Brian Pegg? A really nice boke. Worth going to Sheringham on a cold day for a mardle with him."

ANCIENT FEET (2014) — We're told the earliest evidence of human footprints outside Africa have been discovered at Happisburgh. A series of 800,000-years-old footprints left by humans were uncovered by a team of scientists last May in the ancient estuary mud. They were exposed at low tide as the sea washed away sand to expose long hollows cut into the compacted silts. The prints ranged in size and scientists say they were left by adults and children. The big discovery is announced as part of a new exhibition at the Natural History Museum.

PLAYGROUND CLOCK (2015) — A special clock is unveiled at Sedgeford Primary School to mark its 175th anniversary. The flower-shaped timepiece designed by the pupils is on an outside wall overlooking the playground. In place of numbers, the clock has animals and other favourite objects the youngsters chose to draw. These were then taken to a local blacksmith to be made.

CLUB STALWART (2016) — He's been player, linesman, referee, groundsman, secretary, committee member — and even helped his wife make sandwiches. Malcolm Partridge now notches up a remarkable 70th year connected with Poringland Football Club. The 81-year-old made his debut in the boys' team in 1947 and his senior debut five years later, playing as a wing-half for 21 years.

BIGGER BUZZ (2016) — I can't help wondering what on earth is happening to our lovely language. I've just read that a scheme to "bring a bigger buzz to Dereham" by attracting new businesses to the town centre is set for an April launch. Here's the really good bit from the Eastern Daily Press: "This week, Breckland Council cabinet members supported the eligibility criteria and zones for a pilot discretionary business rates relief scheme." Sheer excitement ...

MARCH

SLIDE RULE (1984) — Annie Adcock of Beetley wins a slide projector for Litcham High School with this witty slogan:" I think slides are an excellent technology aid because they improve the eye-cue!"

TOEING THE LINE (1985) — Budget Day. I miss the Chancellor's speech because of a visit to the chiropodist in an attempt to have ingrowing toenails sorted. Now I can bounce along in the sleet and rain like a modern Gene Kelly. On to join an Any Questions? panel at the Castle Hotel in Norwich. One of those richly-varied days that seem out of harmony with the predictable nature of another Budget. Beer, wine, spirits and cigarettes all up.

FINAL TRIBUTE (1986) — A donkey pulls the coffin to Forncett St Peter Church in a humble cart as a last tribute to his master. Arthur Peacock, 72, of Valley Farm, Forncett St Mary, loved horses and kept 32 ponies as well as the donkey. Son Richard says it was one of his wishes to be taken to his funeral this way. "He'd had the donkey since it was a foal."

CAMPUS SOLUTION? (1987) — Proposals to dump low-level radioactive waste at a rubbish tip in Costessey are given a resounding "No!" by villagers. At a packed public meeting, speakers condemn the controversial plans to dispose of the material from the University of East Anglia. "Why not dig a hole in the university campus and bury it there?" suggests one speaker.

HALF MEASURES (1988) — Overheard in a Norfolk village pub as a farmworker chats with the landlady. She says how cold it's been: "That old wind has been sharp enough to cut you in half." He replies: "Wish it had." After a pause he adds: "Then I would've hed someone ter talk to!"

BACKWATER BASH (1988) — Despite all the pushing, Norfolk continues to enjoy a backwater image. Actor John Sessions joins the fray on Radio 4's Start the Week programme when asked for his impression of Canada: "It's like a sort of concussed Sweden crossed with Norfolk on a Thursday". Well, that used to be early-closing day.

DAFT DINING (1989) — Christmas comes early — or late — for a Great Yarmouth hotel. Regulars sit down to a full traditional Christmas dinner complete with turkey, pudding and crackers. This daft dining at the Duke's Head Hotel is in aid of Comic Relief and raises about £500.

ROYAL HELP (1990) — The Queen is to pay the poll tax for more than 100 workers on her Sandringham estate, as well as their wives and husbands, at a cost of about £56,000. Buckingham Palace confirms the Queen will pay the tax for staff at Sandringham and Balmoral, her private estates, because she does not want workers to suffer financially. Other major Norfolk landowners praise the royal gesture — but say they can't afford to follow suit.

BELL TOLLS (1990) — Brisley Bell, one of my favourite watering-holes, is about to close. Landlady Ada Gricks is pulling her final pints at a pub where fruit machines, disco music and rowdy customers never darkened the door. Parts of the pub date back to 1500 and it was originally a beer house. A bar was installed for the first time in 1966. Before that beer was carried from the cellar down a long passage and served in the kitchen. When Ada and husband Henry leave to live in a bungalow at North Elmham she will be tearing herself away from the place where she was born in 1900. I recall such a homely welcome on several visits with Caister to play the village cricket team. Over the green and into the pub as stumps were drawn. The sun dipping as we tasted a rare bit of old Norfolk. We shall never enjoy anything like that again.

Ada and Henry Grix, long-time hosts at the delightfully old-fashioned Brisley
Bell before the pub closed in 1990.

FARM EQUALITY (1990) – The milkmaid and the cowman disappear – to be replaced by herdspersons. Sex equality leads to a new organisation for the livestock industry called the Professional Herdsperson's Society. An Eastern Daily Press editorial puts the matter in perspective : "Let women achieve equality on the farms. But let 'herdsperson' quickly be lost along with 'spokesperson' and 'chair' in the manure of history."

LYNG MARATHON (1991) – Elsie Cole decides to call it a day 70 years after joining the parochial church council at Lyng. "I think the time has come to hand over to a younger person" says Elsie, who has lived nearly all of her 86 years in the village. Mind you, she likes to see the world and is preparing for her 20th trip to America, flying off to see her rector son in Pennsylvania. Elsie's father was a church warden in Lyng.

TON-UP SNOOZE! (1991) — Sam Flogdell celebrates his 100th birthday just up the road at the British Legion's Halsey House residential home in Cromer. He's enjoying a well-deserved nap when I drop in to pass on congratulations. This must be the first time I've seen a centenarian having a doze just as he reaches three figures! I chatted to him yesterday on my BBC Radio Norfolk Dinnertime Show-because today's schedule (March 26th) is such a busy one for Sam.

SENSITIVE SOUL (1992) — Heavy showers about and a woman offers a lift as I leave the house. She's a truly sensitive soul. "I won't drop you off at that supermarket you don't like next to the railway station. I'll leave you near the Methodist Church" she says. Very thoughtful — and it shows how you can earn a reputation in this job!

SPEAK UP, DOC! (1993) — My birthday celebrations begin with a visit to the doctor's surgery in Cromer as my ears continue to give trouble. My attendance is eagerly seized upon by a nurse who gives me a tetanus injection and a general MOT. I enjoy trying to explain to Dr Ding what the Norfolk expression "ding o'the lug" means. He chuckles and suggests Norfolk people do have some funny little ways.

JESUS ON BIKE (1994) — Palm Sunday celebrations don't quite follow biblical lines in Attleborough when Jesus swaps his four-legged mount for two wheels. The lack of a donkey means there are few smiles and raised eyebrows as Jesus — alias lay reader Russell Davies — rides his bike at the head of the procession to St Mary's parish church. The rector, the Rev John Aves, explains the donkey which usually led Attleborough processions had retired — and the intended replacement had died.

DOGGED BY MESS (1995) — Children at a Norfolk primary school are having daily shoe inspections — because dirty dogs are fouling local streets. Filthy pavements outside North Walsham First School means teachers now check pupils' shoes before allowing them into the classroom. This is a last resort to stave off a health hazard and another indictment of the way many dog owners show no sense of responsibility.

WALLACE AT HOME (1996) — Wallace Walpole celebrates his 100th birthday in the same Garvestone house where's he's lived for almost 80 years. He began working on the railways as a plate layer and went on to do the same for the British Army in France during the First World War. He survived being gassed during his service. He was an ARP warden in his home village during the last war.

ELECTION BAN (1997) — The Lifeboat Inn at Thornham, near Hunstanton, is declared a General Election-free zone. A list of fines is drawn up to penalise any customer showing even a passing interest in the subject. It's all in a good cause, the RNLI, and charges will stay in force until polling day, May 1st. The punishment list ranges from 20p for a mere mention of the unmentionable to £100 for the heinous crime of being a party leader. George Watson, one of the pub regulars, reckons political discussion "upsets the drinking."

MYSTERY BONANZA (1998) — Churchwarden Pat Parsons can hardly believe her eyes – £10,000 in cash stuffed through her letter-box! Worshippers at Outwell, near Downham Market, are delighted by the generous gesture intended for repairs to the parish church roof. But they're all asking the same question — who has given the money? The mystery windfall in £10 notes has been put in several large envelopes with a message saying simply:" For Pat, for the church roof."

WRONG COURSE (1999) — Chaos at Fakenham Races as punters miss out on the chance of a jackpot of almost £700,000. In an unprecedented turn of events, the Conditional Jockeys' Maiden Hurdle is declared void after all 11 runners are disqualified for taking the wrong course. The stewards' decision to annul the race, final event of the day, sparks confusion among the 2,750-strong crowd denied a chance to take the pay-out from the bumper Tote pool worth £682,937. Long queues form at the on-course Tote office as disappointed punters wait for a refund following the controversial verdict.

GATES GONE (2000) — Residents at Horningtoft, near Fakenham, are flabbergasted by the theft of two solid oak gates from the back entrance to the village church. The theft is discovered by Maurice Reeder, who hand-carved the splendid gates in 1981. He says "They were there when I drove past the church at 11 on Friday morning. When I came back, they'd gone. I would imagine they were stolen to order and they would have needed a van to take them away"

FAREWELL IDA (2001) — Norfolk's oldest resident, Ida Wrench, dies at the age of 109. She lived in three centuries and collected nine messages from the Queen. Ida was born in Attleborough in 1891. She married her late husband Henry in 1922 and they had four sons and two daughters. One of Ida's earliest memories was of the Boer War.

HOME TRUTHS (2002) — Intriguing dip into "Chelsea-on-Sea" waters. I'm invited to give a talk in Burnham Market Village Hall to raise funds for Burnham Westgate Church. I keep it fairly light-hearted but take the opportunity to emphasise how local youngsters are being forced out of their own villages by inflated house prices, especially in sought-after areas like the Burnhams. One "adopted local" tells me after the talk: "We have nobs. We have snobs. We have the salt of the earth — true locals — and the weekenders, about whom most of us know nothing." An unsolicited summary of great succinctness!

KNIGHT SERVICE? (2003) — All that remains of Mileham Castle is a grassy mound topped by crumbling masonry. But that hasn't stopped the BBC's licensing chiefs pursuing castle owner, Richard Butler-Stoney, for a colour TV licence fee for the ruin. He's now received a second reminder. Mr Butler-Stoney lives across the road from the castle's remains. A BBC spokesman says Mileham Castle has been on its computer database — although there's no explanation as to how it got there.

JUST IN CASE (2004) — The historic market crosses and humble bus shelters of Norfolk don't seem to be major terrorist targets. Even so, one local council decides to take out insurance against an attack — just in case. North Walsham town councillors agree to pay an extra £105 a year on top of their usual £3,400 insurance cover to include terrorism risk. Insurers advise councils and businesses across the nation to look at the terrorism risk after escalating attacks on "soft" targets.

COOL DOVES (2005) — From a review in the Eastern Daily Press: "Playing as tight as a camel's nostrils in a sandstorm, 21st century rockers Doves produced what must surely be one of this year's highlights at the UEA last night."

FRISKY START (2006) — March comes in more like a growling and scowling polar bear than a lion. Even so, I'm determined to get some exercise and fresh air. I crunch my way through snow and ice along the seafront and up to the clifftop walk towards the lighthouse. Few people about to share such bracing conditions but I really savour the stroll.

ROYAL SMILE (2007) — Proud family day as I receive my MBE from the Queen at Buckingham Palace for services to the Norfolk community. She refers to my journalism with the Eastern Daily Press and writing in the local dialect. She says she finds that difficult to read. I tell her I tend to write it very slowly so it's not too hard to understand. Her Majesty smiles approvingly.

FIRST COUNCIL (2008) — A seaside village is to elect its own parish council for the first time. The parish of Walcott has been created following a boundary review by North Norfolk District Council. A poll will be held on May 1st to elect nine councillors to serve until 2011.Up to now, Walcott has been part of the parish of Happisburgh.

MASTER AT WORK (2009) — Veteran comedian Ken Dodd attracts an inevitable full house at the Pavilion Theatre on Cromer Pier — and I feel truly tickled to see him on stage for the first time. His marathon stint starts at 7pm and he reluctantly lets us out for good behaviour at 12.50am. Good to catch this comedy legend in top form despite a chesty cold. "I should have paid the congestion charge" he quips.

LOCAL FLAVOUR (2010) — Full house at the Fairland Hall as I enjoy a mardle with the Wymondham Born and Bred Club. I salute their brand of proud parochialism in a rapidly-changing Norfolk, especially in a town where developers are waiting eagerly to fill even more fields on the edges with housing. Hard to know now where Wymondham begins and ends.

BACK TO SCHOOL (2011) – Police officers in Thetford are going back to school in a bid to improve community relations. Portuguese lessons are starting for those who would like to learn basic policing terms in that language. It's aimed at helping to break down barriers in the town.

STEWART CLOSE (2012) – A new housing development named after American actor and airbase commander James Stewart is opened in a south Norfolk village. Five affordable homes for local people in Tibenham are opened by Saffron Housing Trust. The project at Stewart Close is named after James Stewart, based at nearby Tibenham Airfield with the USAAF 445th Bombardment Group during the Second World War.

RENE'S MARATHON (2013) – Rene Warner, a church organist for the past 82 years, 75 of them at Trunch Methodist Church, dies at 93. She was also local correspondent for the North Norfolk News for 40 years. Clearly a mawther made for the long haul!

STILL FLYING (2013) – An elderly avocet returns home to its Norfolk birthplace – 23 years after it was first recorded there. The bird, ringed at Titchwell Marsh on July 2nd, 1990, is spotted on the same RSPB reserve, making it one of the oldest avocets ever recorded in the United Kingdom. The species has an average life-span of just seven years.

DURABLE CHARACTER (2014) – Gordon Bailey, Litcham sub-postmaster and shopkeeper for over 40 years, dies at 96. So we say farewell to one of our most cheerful and durable village character who delivered weekly groceries to our Beeston home when I was a lad. Gordon's legs were among the first I spied outside the family circle as I played under the kitchen table. He would bend down and ask if I had been a good boy. He never waited for the answer.

FOND AWARD (2014) – Proud day unfolds at Hingham as I'm one of a group to be awarded life membership of Friends Of Norfolk Dialect – the organisation I set up in 1999. Current chairman Ted Peachment – a fellow old pupil of Hamond's Grammar School in Swaffham – makes the presentations in front of a big gathering at the Lincoln Hall. Local historian Neil Storey gives an illustrated talk on Norfolk in the First World War.

If you're a native of Litcham then you'll have known Gordon Bailey, here standing in the doorway of the emporium and post office.

RED FACE DAY (2015) — A Red Nose Day fundraiser is told it is no laughing matter after his soldier costume leads to a police manhunt across Norwich. The man is caught on video walking around the city dressed as a soldier and holding what appears to be a rifle. His appearance prompts several calls and armed police and a helicopter are called to the city centre. After almost a six-hour search, police track the man down to find he's a charity fundraiser in fancy dress.

CAMERON CLANGER (2016) — Prime Minister David Cameron declares his love for the coast at "Holcombe" in an article for the Eastern Daily Press extolling the virtues of holidaying in Norfolk. It's all part of English Tourism Week. We think Mr Cameron means "Holkham".

APRIL

QUIET TIMES (1985) – Succinct report in the *Eastern Daily Press* from Wighton, near Wells: "No members of the public were at the parish meeting. Mr Seaman, chairman, said the village cemetery was in good order. No money available to buy a grasscutter for general use in the village."

WHISKY GALORE! (1986) – Norfolk lifeboatmen can look forward to a warmer homecoming after cold sea voyages. Every year, John Youngs, who lives in San Francisco, sends 200 bottles of whisky to England to be shared out between lifeboat stations around the country. This time the beneficiaries are Wells, Sheringham, Cromer and Yarmouth. It all started when Mr Youngs visited Norfolk and got to know the Cromer crew.

EGGSENTRIC ROBIN (1987) – A Norfolk robin seems to have got her seasons muddled. She's laid her eggs in a Christmas wreath of holly and roses at Mattishall. It's hanging in Terry Chapman's garage.

CHURNING IT OUT (1988) – A boyhood dream turns to reality – thanks to the contents of an old milk churn. Diss businessman Peter Gillings started to put small change in the churn 25 years ago in a long-term bid to own a new Harley Davidson motor cycle. He takes delivery now of the £8,000 machine after emptying contents of the churn on the sales floor of East Anglian dealers Victoria Motor Company. A local bank manager is on hand to sort out the money. The bike would have cost £430 in 1963.

LUCKY DOVES (1989) – When three-and-a-half year old Joan Boardman launched a Broads wherry at Reedham in 1905, two white doves were released to bring the vessel luck. Little did that little girl know that 84 years later she would come again and set free two more doves to mark the relaunch of the wherry *Hathor*, now restored to her original grandeur.

NO KIDDING! (1989) — Bill the billy goat makes history in East Anglia as the first kid to be born by artificial insemination. The young Anglo-Nubian kid is born at Saxlingham Nethergate. Jean Weeding keeps three pedigree goats and decides to use the latest technology.

HIS LORDSHIP (1990) – A mystery buyer pays over £18,000 for the right to own shipwrecks washed up on his local beach. The unnamed bidder snaps up the Lordship of the Manor of Happisburgh, a title dating back to Edward the Confessor's time.

With the erosion at Happisburgh, we can say with certainty that today's beach is some distance from that owned by the first Lord of the Manor!

CRUEL DILEMMA (1991) — Visit to Sedgeford for a mardle with local Women's Institute members. An illuminating session at the end as we discuss the changing face of Norfolk life. Several newcomers offer their views and one points to a cruel dilemma — "If you don't join in, you are stand-offish. If you do join in, you can stand accused of trying to take over!" A woman who moved from near Heathrow Airport to Syderstone says she and many others have no desire to change Norfolk.

PEASANT HUNTING? (1991) — I'm asked to comment on a Norwich hotel's idea of a £75.50 weekend break to give guests a quick lesson in Norfolk dialect, followed by an eavesdropping trip into the countryside to hear the accent in everyday use. My verdict? Revolting! "This county is not a zoo. The next stop will be setting up a Norfolk wildlife park full of peasants so people can come and stare. Peasant-hunting is a new blood sport the county can do without."

LET THERE BE ... (1992) – "Blind Sam" has his light restored. The lantern, erected at Holt in 1887 to celebrate Queen Victoria's golden jubilee, was christened "Blind Sam" because it was out more often than on. After the First World War it was moved from the Market Place to its present position on Obelisk Plain to make way for the war memorial and it was during this period the lamp disappeared from its support. Holt History Group decide to restore the lantern and members gather around the ornate structure to celebrate its return.

STAR STANLEY (1993) – Stanley Beckham retires after 51 years at Dereham trailer firm Crane Fruehauf – a company record that cannot be repeated. Stanley, 65, joined the firm the day before his 14th birthday. With present employment laws setting minimum and maximum working years, his length of service is unique.

INSIDE JOB (1994) – Ingoldisthorpe village sign will soon be back to its former glory – thanks to the efforts of inmates of Wayland Prison, near Watton. The decorative wooden sign is one of the latest from the area to be sent to jail for a facelift and fresh lick of paint.

TALK IT OVER (1995) – A new scheme at Thetford is intended to take the heat out of neighbourhood rows by sitting enemies in the same room – and making them talk. The proposed mediation service is the brainchild of the Citizen's Advice Bureau, Peddars Way Housing Association and Breckland Council. One of the organisers says: "We had one neighbourhood dispute which actually ended in murder, and it was a dog barking that sent the offender over the edge."

GREY SUPERSTAR (1996) – Sporting legend Desert Orchid thrills thousands of horse-racing fans at Fakenham. At first it seems the grey superstar is just out for an afternoon stroll when he makes a guest appearance. But, right on cue, he's off at a gallop down the racecourse at the point-to-point meeting. A sparkling career included the Cheltenham Gold Cup, Irish Grand National and Whitbread Gold Cup. He also won four National Hunt Horse of the Year awards.

FRY LINKS (1997) — A plaque in memory of prison reformer Elizabeth Fry is unveiled on the Cromer path she used to walk. The memorial is placed in the picturesque Links Wood where she spent time with her Quaker family, the Gurneys. It's unveiled by town and district councillor Vera Woodcock, determined these links with Cromer should not be forgotten. Five years ago she was instrumental in the move to name the nearby Happy Valley to Overstrand Road path Elizabeth Fry Walk.

BOGUS ACCENTS (1998) — A busy St George's Day defending the proper Norfolk accent. The Channel 4 television programme *Right to Reply* heads for Cromer after complaints about bogus local tones on the legal drama *Kavanagh QC*, starring John Thaw. Last week's episode was set in Norfolk, much of it filmed in the shadow of Norwich Cathedral, and several characters were supposed to be locals. We got the usual Mummerzet mixture. Protests went in. Channel 4 comes out to talk to folk affected. I emphasise how often our Norfolk dialect has been mocked in this way over many years.

PARISH SLUMP (1999) — An influx of newcomers, an absence of young blood and lack of interest in local issues are blamed for a slump in the numbers entering parish politics. Election registration officials report a decline in people seeking election to parish councils. On average, just 30 per cent of Norfolk parishes will go to the polls this year. There are no candidates in Sandringham, Holkham, South Pickenham and Southery.

VIVE THE DIALECT! (2000) — A record entry and big audience for the annual Norfolk dialect celebration in Cromer Parish Hall as I adjudicate for the 18th successive year. And there's an intriguing contribution from a French woman, Dominique Ward, from Mundesley way. She earns a distinction certificate for her wry efforts — and plenty of extra publicity locally and nationally for the cultural cause.

*Vera Woodcok, MBE, of Cromer, instrumental in setting up the memorial to
Elizabeth Fry at Cromer, just one of her many achievements in over 60 years on
the Urban District and then the Town Council*

CAUGHT IN ACT (2001) — A barmaid who used her handbag to floor a would-be mugger is left stunned herself — after discovering the "thief" is an actor! Nicola Hughes spots a man snatching the handbag of an elderly woman in Norwich's Anglia Square. She's outraged as he runs by and clubs him over the head so hard that the handles break on her bag. Unfortunately, the man left sprawled on the pavement with a bloodied nose and dazed expression by this public-spirited act is not the villain he seems but an actor taking part in a reconstruction. His "crime" is being filmed for Anglia TV's *Crimenight* programme by a camera crew obscured by a bus shelter.

MISERABLE LOT! (2002) — Scruffy and grumpy old men who rarely smile ... that's how the nation's children see Britain's farmers, according to a new poll. But local farmers — and their children — hit back by saying they feel the poll's findings bear little relation to their own experiences.

BACK TOGETHER (2003) — Evening trek to the Thomas Paine Hotel in Thetford for a gathering of local Rotarians past and present. My first newspaper mentors, Jim Wilson and John Kitson, are there to hear me sing for my supper. First time, methinks, we've been together under the same roof for over 40 years.

MIDWIFE MADGE (2004) — A small woman who spent her working life as a midwife in rural Norfolk dies at 100. Nurse Madge Spence lived in Field Dalling and worked as the area midwife for over 40 years. Lindy Green of Wighton describes her as "strict but always very kind, caring and funny." She helped deliver Mrs Green's second daughter. "Madge Spence was only knee-high to a grasshopper. She had bright rouged cheeks and a cackling laugh we can hear even now."

SPRING CLEAN (2007) — Old furniture, old clutter — and even a church organ — pile up on the streets of Cobholm, in Great Yarmouth, as locals discard more than 20 tonnes of household rubbish in a pioneering resident-led spring clean. While environmental action days take place regularly, this is the first to be organised by the community. There are hopes it can be a model for future schemes across the county.

YOU ARE JOKING! (2009)– Yet another of those infernal surveys says Norwich is the most humourless place in the United Kingdom, a city where people are least likely to crack a joke, break into fits of giggles or look on the funny side of life. The sad statistic is met with scorn by Norwich folk, including old friend Olly Day. He leaps to the city's defence and champions its distinctive wry sense of humour and voracious appetite for stand-up comedy. Norwich comes last in a league of 30 towns and cities.

CLASS PERFORMER (2011) — She's lived in the village all her 91 years and was a pupil at the local school — and her mother was a teacher there almost 110 years ago. And Joan Smith proves the real star of the day as she officially opens a new classroom at Great Dunham Primary School. The sprightly special guest captivates the youngsters as she recalls what life was like at the Victorian school during her time there in the 1930s. Her mother, Laura Whales, taught at the school from 1902. To avoid accusations of favouritism, Mrs Smith started her education at Fransham and Lexham before taking her seat at Dunham.

SOGGY RECORD (2012) — The wettest April in 100 years — and the Badminton Horse Trials are off at the end of the month because of a waterlogged course. "Devastating!" exclaim the event organisers. Even so, there are bigger worries in other parts of the country where rain continues to pelt down.

PAYING UP (2013) — A touching incident amid sunswept mardling at Cromer's outdoor market. I'm buying fruit and vegetables when a woman customer next to me opens her purse and asks me to accept a £10 note. Apparently, she had an item from me about seven years ago when she attended a talk I was giving — but had forgotten to pay. I tell her to put it in her local church coffers and thank her for such honesty. "Now I can talk to you again with a clear conscience!" she sighs on leaving the scene.

TITANIC MENU (2014) — A second-class breakfast menu from the doomed ship *Titanic* sells at auction for a remarkable £87,000. Perhaps inclusion of a Norfolk delicacy, lovely Yarmouth bloaters, helps push up the bidding. The menu, which doubled as a postcard, is among memorabilia from the Titanic being auctioned to mark the 102nd anniversary of the sinking.

PERFECT DATE (2015) — Dispensing Norfolk squit on All Fools' Day seems highly appropriate — and so I relish a chance to entertain a large and receptive gathering of Starting Handle Club enthusiasts at Bawburgh Village Hall. We arrive early and so enjoy a refreshing drink beforehand in Barford Cock. A chap comes in with boxes of kitchen knives to sell and we're among those to decline his offer. I recall in the "old days" how Friday night callers at local pubs included shellfish purveyors with baskets under their arms.

RICH CYCLE (2015) — A teenage romance blossomed into a life-long love for Norfolk couple Nigel and Grace Etheridge after they met in a bike shop. The couple from Lingwood now have cause for celebration as they mark 70 years of marriage. The platinum pair first met at their local bike shop in Cantley when they were 14.

FINAL CURTAIN (2016) — Playwright Sir Arnold Wesker dies at 83. He put Norfolk on an international stage with his play Roots. I was his host and inquisitor in 1984 when BBC Radio Norfolk initiated a Wesker Week, a salute inspired to a large extent by his friendship with news editor Ian Hyams. Wesker could be a prickly customer but I got to like him after a full week of programmes and events. He returned a few years on to plug his autobiography, *As Much as I Dare*. He worked at the Bell Hotel in Norwich as a porter in the 1950s and married Dusty, a girl from Starston.

WHOLE TOOTH (2016) — It looks like an odd-shaped stone. But a lump of rock discovered on the north Norfolk coast is identified as the tooth of a creature which last roamed the earth 700,000 years ago — the mammoth. Treasure hunter Nigel Thorogood makes the discovery while combing the beach at West Runton.

MAY

THICK AND THIN (1986) — "People do extraordinary things to raise money" says Diss solicitor Irene Jacoby. She and dentist Adrian Kinnear-King are sticking to their diets through thick and thin to raise money for a community centre scheme for Diss. She is trying to lose three stones. He hopes to put on several pounds with a sponsored weight increase!

WIDE AWAKE (1986) – Telling a Sunday newspaper that it's not so sleepy as the image created by one of its television adverts has earned Little Snoring a £100 donation to its village hall and playing field fund. The money comes from the Mail on Sunday.

UGLY CONTEST (1987) — "Belton is the ugliest village in Norfolk" claims Great Yarmouth councillor Cora Batley. Discussing a plan to landscape an area in the village, she tells the borough council's development control sub-committee "I think it needs more trees and more grass in that area. I would have thought people would be only too pleased to have an open space with grass, seeds and trees." Bill Dougal interjects: "I think Hemsby is the ugliest village." The committee approves the improvement scheme.

SPECIAL BOX (1988) – A building with standing room for only two people is officially listed to be preserved. The oldest Automobile Association telephone box in East Anglia, at Brancaster Staithe, is confirmed as a grade-two listed building. The sentry-style black box, standing in a lay-by off the A149, is more than 30 years old and one of just a few originals left in working order in the country.

JENNY WEIGHS IN (1989) — Little Jenny Cloke must be the youngest church benefactor on record. She was helping St Mary's at Ditchingham to raise funds even before she was born. When she arrives the church collects £65 from parishioners and others who took part in a "guess the baby's weight" competition. She weighs in at a healthy 7lb, 13 and a half ounces and the money will help fund church repairs needed after the 1987 gales. Pauline Reeder, of Broome, wins a bottle of mature brandy given by the Rector, the Rev Roger Holmes, for guessing the right weight.

JUST THE TICKET (1990) — Churchwardens interrupt the service at North Walsham parish church — to present the vicar, the Rev Martin Smith, with tickets for a trip to Italy to mark his 25th anniversary as a priest. A standing ovation follows from the congregation.

BETTER FOR IT! (1990) – A lovely warm day shared with son Danny on and round Cromer beach. We look around the lifeboat and wander up and down the pier, so much more appealing since gale-force winds removed the amusement arcade! It has not been replaced — and the vast majority of locals suggest it's all the better for that! Yes, a predominately older set use the pier, probably because it evokes memories of a more genteel age, but their comments do match what I'm coming to know as the Cromer mood.

HANDY OASIS (1991) — Pleasantly surprised at some aspects of Yarmouth's gearing up for the new holiday season. For example, pedestrianisation of the market place makes a telling difference. Busy but not too brash and a bit of an oasis in the middle of so much traffic.

HEADLINE HITS (1992) — Fascinating chat on the wireless with Robin Limmer, just retired after more than 40 years on the Eastern Daily Press. He also bows out as the last Norfolk-born sub-editor on the paper. Robin's lasting claim to fame is his large collection of amusing headlines culled from those years of creativity. My favourites include "Old Soldiers Go Back to Front" and "Motorist Kicked in Bollards". He also shares several that didn't get into print!

DIALECT LIVES! (1993) – A survey shows many adults do have a strong grasp of our local dialect vocabulary. The Eastern Daily Press also shows youngsters fare better than expected, with Thetford pupil Amy Chrystal scoring 17 out of 20 when confronted by a list of dialect words. Language expert Professor Peter Trudgill, from Norwich, says the survey confirms there is a future for the Norfolk dialect. "Norfolk people will always be speaking in a way which distinguishes them from London and the Midlands."

Professor Peter Trudgill, Eastern Daily Press columnist on Mondays and liguistic expert – as well as having all 16 great-grandparents born and bred in Norfolk.

BURIED LEISURE (1995) – Naughty bedtime stories penned by Norfolk-born author Brian Aldiss are unearthed in a wood at the Devon boarding school where he buried them well over 50 years ago. Brian, 69, says he hid them in a biscuit tin down a rabbit hole to escape a beating because they were saucy. As they come to light, sixth-formers who find them describe the work by the author, who was born and lived at East Dereham as a child, as "zany and gory – with lots of violence."

RAMBLING ON (1996) – George le Surf, founder member of the 4,000 strong Norfolk Ramblers' Association, retires as secretary – but has no intention of ending his rambling days. The 75-year-old says "There's no finer way to see the countryside than walking." When he came to Norfolk in the 1950s he noticed the low standard of footpaths and hostility of landowners.

REOPENING TIME (1997) – Parishioners in a tiny Norfolk village celebrate the reopening of their church which closed 14 years ago amid safety concerns. Many of the 30 residents of Illington, near

Thetford, help to fill St Andrew's Church for the first service of a new era following restoration work costing £55,000. The small medieval church was closed when the tower became so dangerous it was feared it might collapse.

FLYING PLAGUE (1998) — A plague of flies named after a saint is swarming across the region. Clouds of black St Mark's flies are reported in one of the worst infestations for a decade. Black hordes of these harmless flies are spotted hovering in lanes and roads and around woodland feeding on fresh greenery in the countryside. Named after St Mark the Evangelist, these flies lie dormant during winter in the soil of uncultivated fields.

CLOSE OF PLAY (1999) — A veteran Norfolk village cricketer dies at the beloved club ground where he piled up impressive statistics in more than 40 seasons of playing. Tony Curson, 71, has a heart attack while mowing the pitch where he'd performed for Hethersett 24 hours earlier. He'd returned to prepare the wicket for a forthcoming series of fixtures for youth and B teams. In his 45 years with Hethersett as a player, Tony, a past captain and current secretary, scored more than 23,000 runs, took 2,600 wickets and held about 700 catches. A proud servant.

HEARTY MABEL (2000) — Mabel Howard proves life can be improved — even at the age of 107! The Norfolk centenarian becomes the oldest person in Britain to have a pacemaker fitted. Mabel is given a new lease of life at Papworth Hospital, near Cambridge, just before her birthday and says "You're only as old as you feel." Born in 1893 in Castle Acre, she now lives in a residential home in Swaffham. Doctors marvel at her strength and say they had no hesitation in going ahead with the lifesaving operation. Daughter Sandra says: "She usually takes things in her stride and with a smile on her face."

GEMMA'S JACKPOT (2003) — As a teenager, Gemma Burtenshaw would spend freezing winter mornings delivering papers to earn some money. Today the 21-year-old returns to the Norwich newsagent's where she used to work — to collect her £167,252 lottery winnings.

Bill Bird — the inspiration behind the Tunstead Trosh.

LONG CLOSURE (2004) — The heart of Mileham in mid-Norfolk is to be shut off for five months to extend the mains sewerage system. The B1145 through the village will close on June 14th and is not due to reopen until November.

BACK IN FOLD (2005) — Veteran local football reporter Roy Webster is allowed back into Wroxham's ground after 205 days of being shut out. The colourful character, with his trademark beard and hat, was forced to report on Wroxham fixtures from a ladder pitched against a wall of the Trafford Park ground. He was banned over what the club regarded as "adverse articles" but is back in his normal seat for the end-of-season clash with Harwich & Parkeston after a truce is called.

PULLING TOGETHER (2006) — Little Snoring has seen a transformation in crime levels and the atmosphere of the village, thanks to youngsters, older people and the local authorities all pulling together. Norfolk Rural Community Council says it hopes this shining example of making life better for everyone could be used as a blueprint to tackle problems in other communities.

WONDERBIRDS ARE GO! (2007) — With its moss-turfed roof and sheer glass front, this futuristic building looks like something out of Thunderbirds. But this is more like "Wonderbirds" because the space-age creation, which could be a secret enemy hideaway that has whirred out of the ground, is the new base for a rather less sinister group — wildlife fans. After years of planning and months of work, the new £1m visitor centre overlooking Cley Marshes opens its doors.

MEADOW MISERY (2008) —A shocking new report reveals that nearly 70pc of meadows in Norfolk are in a poor or declining condition with one in 10 no longer attractive to wildlife. Hideous blot on our green credentials.

STEAM SALUTE (2009) — Bill Bird would have puffed out his chest with pride at the sight of old gems steaming past. A procession of steam-powered vehicles winds through the north Norfolk countryside to salute the man behind one of the region's favourite nostalgia events. Bill Bird, who died in 2007, was one of the founders of the

Tunstead Trosh, which taught thousands of people about traditional farming techniques. The North Norfolk Steam Tour, organised by the East Anglian Traction Engine Society, sets out from the Thursford Collection — and passes Bill's old home at Tunstead.

CENTURY UP (2010) — Letheringsett Village Hall marks its 100th anniversary with a music hall-style celebration. This quaint brick and flint building was given as a lending library by the local squire in Edwardian times. Former ITN political editor and village hall trust chairman Michael Brunson leads the festivities. He now lives locally.

ENID'S DAY (2012) — A popular centenarian opens a May Day fete which marks a community tradition going back hundreds of years. Retired headteacher Enid Lilley does the honours on her 100th birthday, arriving at Shipdham's Drynklings event on the village green by horse and cart in a procession from All Saints' Church. The Drynklings fete was restarted 12 years ago and always takes place on May Day.

PALIN LINKS (2013) — Monty Python legend and travel documentary maker Michael Palin renews his long-established links with Fakenham as he joins the town's junior school centenary celebrations. His grandfather, Edward Palin, was a doctor in Fakenham and he attended the original ceremony to open Fakenham Junior School on May 21st, 1913. Michael's father was also born in Fakenham.

QUALITY OF LIFE (2014) — Around one home is bought for more than £1m in Norfolk every month — and estate agents believe demand is about to increase. "A lot of our buyers are from London and the Home Counties" says Max Sowerby, who has offices across north Norfolk. "The value of their property has gone up so much that it's given them a lot of confidence to either buy a second home or sell up and do the big move to Norfolk. We may take a gasp at £3m but where a lot of these buyers are coming from, it doesn't get you much. So quality of life is a big differential."

DOUBLE CHEERS (2014) – A pair of identical twins achieve the rare feat of being able to celebrate a 92nd birthday together. Believed to be the oldest surviving identical twins in the country, David and John Smith celebrate in what has become something of a tradition – two pints of Guinness followed by a whisky with family and friends at The Greyhound pub in Swaffham.

EDEN IS CLOSE (2015) – Laughter rings out and friendships are renewed at a Norfolk seaside boarding school reunion with a difference. Pupils and staff from Eden Hall School in Bacton can no longer visit old classrooms as the school was demolished to make way for houses. Instead, they unveil a commemorative plaque on St George's Close, where Eden Hall once stood, and are then treated to a tea party by Close residents. The building dated back to 1899 and became a Norfolk County Council school between 1954 and 1981. It cared for children with health problems.

PEALS APPEAL (2015) – Church bells chime again in a Norfolk village after completion of an eight-year campaign to raise £120,000. The bells of St Mary's Church in North Creake are returned, renewed and added to. Villagers have been raising the money since 2007, running fundraising events and taking in donations and contributions from small charities. Not one penny of the £120,000 has come from a major funding body,

LAST ROUND-UP (2016) – Errol "Cowboy" Crossan, one of the last surviving members of the Norwich City team to reach the 1958-59 FA Cup semi-finals, dies at 85. The Canadian right-winger with his fetching crewcut, played in all 11 games as the Canaries made national headlines by overcoming all the odds to reach the last four as a Third Division side. They were beaten by Luton after a replay. Crossan scored four goals in the run, including one in the 3-0 win over Manchester United at a snowy Carrow Road. I interviewed him on Radio Norfolk when he returned for 25th anniversary celebrations in January, 1984. He shed tears when I played the record Crossan and Bly, written and recorded by my cousin Paul Wyett – and I almost came out in sympathy.

FRESH AND CHIPS (2016) — A day plucked from high November for First of the Summer Chips (Norfolk's answer to Last of the Summer Wine). Old newspaper colleagues Frank Gordon, Colin Bevan and Tom Walshe travel to Cromer for our third tasty reunion on the seafront. Brooding skies, harsh winds and sharp raindrops keep us company on our way to our fish-and-chips bonanza. We sit in the warm, munching, chatting and laughing while angry waves lap around the pier not far away. We give a wander along Cromer's most famous landmark a miss this time.

Day out by the briny for newspaper chums (left to right) Colin Bevan, Frank Gordon and Tom Walshe

FLOATING VOTER? (2016) — A member of Breckland Council's election staff thinks he's landed himself in hot water when he trips and drops a Police and Crime Commissioner ballot box into a pond by his house. It's thought he tripped over his dog, sending him and the ballot box tumbling into the pond. Breckland's returning officer says : "I'm pleased to say the member of election staff involved in the accident was still able to get the box, which did not contain any marked ballot papers, to the polling station in plenty of time."

JUNE

DIALECT DELIGHT (1984) — First day of the Royal Norfolk Show at Costessey and hundreds of Radio Norfolk listeners introduce themselves as I host the Dinnertime Show from Stand 42 (opposite toilets, so we have a sort of captive audience). A real delight to find the most frequently used greeting is "Thanks for what you're doing to help keep our dialect alive." Rather ironic in view of the number of bowler-hatted gents and fashion-conscious ladies giving cut-glass accents an airing!

CARRY ON, CHAPS! (1985) — Government's "Civil Defence and the Farmer" guide is published with up-to-date advice from Whitehall to keep farming going after a nuclear attack. Polythene sheets, a bucket of dirt and an ample supply of straw bales — that's the survival kit.

WILD WEST (1987) — Anglia Television presenter and farmer Dick Joice is the latest victim of a gang of cattle rustlers operating in west Norfolk. The gang steal 22 cattle from his farm at Newton-by-Castle Acre.

POSTER BONANZA (1988) — Posters found beneath Wolferton Station Museum, near Sandringham, raise nearly £78,000 at a London auction. Roger Hedley-Walker discovered the 445 posters hidden by his father around 20 years ago when he lifted floorboards at the museum to create more storage space. Money from the auction will be used for repair work at the museum.

POLITE PLAUDIT (1988) — Norwich is voted the most courteous community in Britain. The Polite Society visited pubs, shops, hotels and public services across the country and dubbed Norwich "the city with a smile." Lord Mayor David Bradford, will be presented with a commemorative silver salver. "We ought to try to live up to our reputation" he says. "It has come as a surprise to me because normally Norfolk people are fairly reserved."

NOBLE EFFORT (1989) — Eveline Noble sits down to a Yarmouth seaside holiday breakfast nearly 90 years after she first visited the resort, The south Londoner started her love affair with the town in 1902 and has holidayed there ever since. She recalls that on her first visit with her parents she sailed up on a paddle steamer from the Thames. But that stopped in 1908 and she started travelling by train.

DAREDEVIL DAVID (1990) —The Rev David Ainsworth is the toast of Northrepps, near Cromer, after plunging from the top of his church tower, watched by scores of cheering parishioners. His sponsored abseil goes without a hitch. Raising money for church repairs, the 61-year-old rector says: "Before I launch myself into eternity, I want to welcome you to this great occasion and I hope you find it highly entertaining." Inside the church, long-serving organist Henry Lloyd is sponsored to spend the day playing his way through all 533 hymns in the church hymn book.

END OF NEWS (1991) — Newsreader John Bacon retires from Anglia Television after 31 years. He presented 16,250 bulletins — that's more than 5,500 hours of broadcasting.

REGAL FAREWELL (1993) — Curtain falls on the Wymondham Regal after nearly 60 years. Film lovers and town residents flock to the 276-seat cinema to watch its grand finale. Lew Mulliner, who was at the Regal's first picture show in 1937, 'Springtime', starring Ginger Rogers, says: "It's a very sad occasion. The Regal will be greatly missed." Manager Les King says the cinema can no longer compete with those in Norwich. He says it was still using the same projection equipment as in 1937.

PUB CHARACTERS (1994) — Old Norwich and some of its characters — like a chap who brought a chicken home from New Zealand — dominate our end-of-week mardle in the Horse and Dray on Ber Street in the city. George, a former boxer, and Clifford, who lost a leg in a work accident 20 years ago, lead the yarn-telling. Bursts of laughter as one tries to top the other. I reckon this is what pubs should be about and this one remains a refuge from the modern storm of fruit machines, satellite television and other instant "entertainment." A new landlord, from Essex, has heeded advice to let the place stay true to its old-fashioned virtues.

TRAIL AND RAIL (1996) — A truly crowning achievement for Coronation Day (June 2nd). I walk the eight miles in the Kelling Hospital Trail and Rail event — and live to tell the tale. Warm sunshine means an all-over tan — that's all over my head — but my legs stand up well to a challenging stroll from the hospital grounds down to Weybourne cliffs and on to Sheringham Park. About 500 on the march and I reckon for some it's a conscience-salver before the Great Summer of Sport prepares a comfortable armchair in front of the television.

SECRET WORLD (1997) — There are certain occasions destined to stand out when it comes to reflecting on the year — and this evening's visit to Guestwick in that "secret" world around Reepham is bound to be on the list. I have the anchor role for a production of All Preachers Great and Small with old friends Brian Patrick and David Woodward. Down winding lanes refreshed by heavy rain, dog-roses climbing into the June spotlight, the church, farm and cluster of housing come as a surprise in the glorious sunshine. The vicar and his wife break into their holiday Scarborough way to join us in St Peter's for a Norfolk village event blessed with a perfect setting.

PETROL FIRST (1998) — A survey carried out by Healthy Norfolk 2000 says people living in rural parts of the county are going without essential healthcare in order to keep their cars running. Lack of public transport is forcing many people to neglect their health and to give up holidays in favour of putting petrol in their tanks.

HOSTAGE PUPILS (1999) — A massive swarm of bees holds hundreds of Norfolk children hostage at school. The "tornado" surrounds a mobile classroom at Millfield Primary in North Walsham.

Around 350 pupils are forced to stay indoors on one of the hottest June days so far. Teachers raise the alarm and keep the youngsters under lock and key for their own safety. Headteacher John Aitken says it's like a scene from a horror film.

LIMP EXCUSE? (2000) — One of the most bizarre items of lost property ever handed in arrives at West Norfolk police station. A false leg and attached pair of blue denim jeans are found, apparently abandoned, in Wiggenhall St Germans.

PERCY TUNES IN (2001) — Memorable night at Bawburgh as I open the new village hall — and Percy Garrod completes a remarkable double. He gave a tune or two on his violin when the former hall was opened 64 years ago. Now he takes centre stage again with his mandolin on another happy and proud occasion. The 91-year-old former teacher, one-time cabinet maker and expert in instrument restoration, earns a rapturous reception for his musical set.

STILL WAITING (2004) — Almost 50 letters sent out by a postal watchdog to East Anglian MPs to complain about reliability of Royal Mail have not yet been delivered — six weeks after they were posted.

PANNING OUT (2005) — A former forester ditches his £38,000 -a-year job to become Britain's first full-time gold prospector! Vince Thurkettle, of Great Hockham, reckons he'll earn about a quarter of his former wage as he sifts through tons of gravel and dirt in rivers in Wales, Scotland and maybe even Ireland for specks of gold. President of the World Gold Panning Association, he says he didn't want to hang about waiting for his pension. He's already been hunting for gold for 30 years in his spare time.

GOLF MARATHON (2006) — Farmer Ian Mason reflects on his remarkable round-Norfolk golf marathon as his fundraising total reaches £50,000. He covers all the county's 31 courses, plays 468 holes and takes 2,258 shots along the way. The 43-year-old farmer from Hillington collects a £3,000 cheque at the Royal Norfolk Show to boost his amount being collected for Macmillan Cancer Support.

Eric Edwards passing on his skills as a reedcutter at his beloved How Hill.

STIRRING THE POT (2007) — The Crab Wars are in serious danger of flaring up again! A council report calls Cromer "an up-and-coming community" while Sheringham is dismissed as "a small, secondary town." It's just a storm in a crabpot, really, but enough people take it seriously to ensure another round of intense local rivalry.

SAM'S PLAQUE (2008) — It's never too late ... 42 years after his death, Great Yarmouth and District Archaeological Society pays tribute to a colourful life by putting up a blue plaque to "Sam Larner, Norfolk Fisherman and Folk Singer" at the Winterton cottage where he lived most of his adult life. Sam was "discovered" in 1956 in a pub by a BBC radio producer from Birmingham who recorded about 25 of his songs.

DOCKING RESCUE (2010) — Evening of drama at Sedgeford Village Hall. I'm here to sing for my supper at a special fundraising event organised by Saving Faces, a charity supporting splendid work by reconstructing doctors. The caterers fail to turn up — and I'm invited to entertain until emergency rations of fish and chips arrive. An order for nearly 90 portions must have sent a shudder of apprehension through the Docking shop where the Sedgeford contingent headed. But the rescue operation is applauded warmly as supper is unwrapped.

YES, IT IS! (2011) — It's pantomime time already in Flitcham. Villagers reckon they're too busy to stage one at Christmas — so they're staging one in June instead. A 26-strong cast takes to the stage at the village school. Retired university lecturer Terry Allen has written the Flitcham Fantasia. He says: "We thought it would be easier to rehearse in the summer. Christmas is a hectic time and trudging through the dark to rehearsals isn't fun." This is the first panto to be performed for seven years in this village on the edge of the Royal Estate.

UP THE CREEK (2012) — Villagers at Burnham Overy Staithe transform a creek into a wicket for a game of cricket to mark the Queen's Jubilee. Allcomers are welcome to face demon bowler Chris Gearing for an innings as he sends a foot-wide tennis ball hurtling towards the oars pressed into service as wickets. As the tide drops in the tiny harbour, exposing a sizeable sandbank, parish councillor Chris wades out to put the stumps next to the grounded Scolt Island ferry.

ERIC'S FAREWELL (2012) — A stormy Broadland backcloth as we say farewell to reed-cutter Eric Edwards in a packed church at Ludham, not far from his beloved How Hill. I can imagine the reeds waving an animated goodbye to this outstanding Norfolk character with a scythe. Over 300 folk pile in to pay respects. Simon Partridge, director of the How Hill Trust, towers over the congregation to pay warm tribute: "Eric loved being on the marshes. He was a lucky man who loved his job. Being thigh-deep in water in the middle of winter would not be considered nice by the average man. But he was not an average man."

IT'S A SCOOP! (2013) — Caped crusaders dish out free dog-poo bags, leaflets and advice outside North Walsham's Milfield Primary School. It's part of the National Big Scoop Day aimed at raising awareness about the anti-social nature of pet fouling. These heroes, dressed in masks and wearing capes emblazoned with the slogan "Be a super pooper scooper!", are really environmental health officers from North Norfolk District Council.

HERE AGAIN! (2014) — Christine and Cliff ring the doorbell. I answer and they say "We were at your wedding!". I tell them the reception ended some time ago. Diane arrives on the scene to greet old friends from Sheffield. They're on holiday in these parts and take a chance on chasing away over 30 years.

DEDICATED DUO (2014) — A dedicated pair of community stalwarts are praised for immeasurable contributions to village life, both devoting 37 years to their local action committee. David Myhill and Peter Bennett step down as chairman and vice-chairman of Yaxham Village Amenities Association, roles they've held since the association was formed in 1977. They've organised countless celebrations in the village near Dereham and overseen construction and extension of the village hall. Although both men are looking forward to more free time during their "retirement", they remain on the committee and have just attended what David calculates to be their 432nd meeting.

TAXING NEWS (2015) — Joy turns to disappointment for thousands of employees after a letter informing them of a tax rebate proves to be a mistake. The majority of 6,000 workers on the Norfolk County Council payroll system were told they had paid too much tax and were said to have received rebates worth up to as much as £800. Now an email from the authority to its staff explains there has been an error. People are advised to bank the money and not spend it until they have to repay the tax at a later date.

STEAM RETURN (2016) — Steam trains are set to return to the main line in Cromer this summer. The special dining-car services are being organised by the North Norfolk Railway which operates the heritage line between the Bittern Line's terminus in Sheringham and neighbouring Holt. First of the new services, starting at Sheringham and running between Cromer and Holt, will operate in August.

Steam up for a trial at Cromer Beach station.

JULY

TOP FIND, BY GUM! (1985) – Miss Marsden's class at the John of Gaunt First School at Aylsham are looking for the owner of a top set of false teeth. One of the pupils, eight-year-old Philip Barrett, found the teeth on a school trip to Holkham Beach. He says: "We are trying to find the person who lost them and ask them to come to the school to fit them. They look quite old and have been in the sea for some time. Someone might have swum out and lost them." And to prove they fit, Philip has a test up his sleeve: "We'll make them eat one of Mrs Cox's delicious cakes." She's the school cook.

GAME WARDEN (1986) – North Norfolk motorists have a cracking time and leave traffic warden Alan Auckland with egg on his face. He takes his turn in the pillory outside the Robin Hood pub in Sheringham to raise money to buy guide dogs for the blind.

KINGS OF CASTLES (1987) – Yarmouth's in just the right mood to shatter a world record by building a three-and-a-half-mile sandcastle. More than 1200 people from all over Norfolk grab buckets and spades for the big dig to earn the town a place in the record books. The result is a huge sand fortress snaking from the Wellington Pier, past the Pleasure Beach and ending near the South Denes caravan camp. It's 18,656 feet long and takes two-and-a-half hours to officially measure with a surveyor's wheel. Entertainer Roy Castle oversees the record attempt. He's the oldest Castle there!

ROUGH INVADER (1987) – Main topic at Diss Golf Club – a streaker bursting out of the rough to put women competing in the president's ladies' day off their stroke. Police rush to the course but the intruder, aged about 17, made good his escape. Club president Eric Wright says: "Unfortunately, nobody got a very good description. He upset one or two ladies."

RAINY REALISM (1988) — Romantic memories of the traditional Sunday School treat are tinged with realism as the rain falls on Brisley Green. Ferried by farm trailer from all over the Brisley and Elmham Deanery, children gather for a picnic and open-air service on the village green. The event goes ahead in the semi-shelter of the cricket pavilion.

PEACE GESTURE (1989) — A council names a street after a scrap dealer who fought them all the way to the High Court and European Court of Human Rights. Richard Drake's old scrap yard at Buxton, near Aylsham, has given way to four executive homes. Broadland District Council is naming the new access road Drake's Lane. But for 12 years the late Mr Drake was locked in a courtroom battle with Broadland over land he owned at Stratton Strawless. It wasn't until 1986 that the council dropped a High Court action against him. His widow Kathleen says it makes a nice peace gesture.

BIRTHDAY PEAL (1990) — Champion fundraiser Carrie Coleman is reduced to tears as she hears news of a special birthday treat. Carrie, 81 later this month, will hear the bells of her beloved Gimingham Parish Church peal properly for the first time in over a century. She started fundraising in 1984. Now, £12,000 later, she's ready for a wonderful birthday peal.

SIGN OF TIMES (1991) — Big news from Sea Palling : "At a meeting of the village hall management committee it was agreed to ban smoking at future Friday night bingo sessions in the hall." It can only be a matter of time before the harassed smoker is forced to join a club to enjoy a furtive puff or two on Thursday evenings!

STUMPED BY MOLES (1992) — A village cricket team is in danger of being bowled out by an army of moles laying siege to their pitch. Cricketers at Filby say the problem is so bad they may well have to declare "we surrender!" It's not unusual for 30 molehills to litter the pitch and every week the creatures get a little closer to the crease. Filby have already been forced out of league cricket by the state of their pitch on the village playing field. Now they have a mountain to climb just to fit in some friendlies.

"SONNY" TOAST (1993) — Villagers raise a glass to the memory of a retired farmer who left all he owned to the rural community he loved. As a final gesture, 84-year-old Lionel "Sonny" Curson of Pentney asks for his land to be left as a sports field and the rest of his estate, between £40,000 and £70,000, to the village. He also leaves £2,000 for the parish church. Over the years he had paid for the village sign and sold off strips of farmland for villagers to buy at low prices after he retired.

FERRET REFUGE (1994) — Unwanted, battered and abandoned ferrets can find a safe haven at a new rescue centre. The man behind the Yarmouth Ferret Appreciation Club declares: "How could anyone mistreat such beautiful animals?" Bryan Witherstone has set up the club and rescue centre at his home in Cobholm.

HE'S A CARD! (1995) — Entertaining missive from Mannington Hall in the shape of a postcard from Lady Walpole. She tells how Robin (Lord Walpole) was looking for an opportunity to ask an old employee if he was thinking of retiring. "We were delighted with his reply:' Time I feel orryte, I'll keep a'cummin'!'. What a cheerful start to the day!

FINAL BELL (1996) — One of Norfolk's oldest and smallest village schools with just nine pupils on the register disappears into history. When Beachamwell County First School opened in 1835 it boasted 100 youngsters. Now residents fear passing of the school marks yet another chapter in the decline of their village which has a population of 200 and has already lost a bakery, garage and shop. They fear the village will fail to attract young families.

HE HAS TO GO! (1997) — A scarecrow is censored at Trunch. The two-dimensional figure which twitches in the wind has taken pride of place on a village allotment for about a month. But now, "Mr Viagra", as dubbed by his creators, faces the chop after some locals are offended by his proportions and call the police. Owners Joan and Allan Jones say they put him up for a giggle and most villagers had laughed along. He's also proved something of a tourist attraction. Police visit the spot and decide he has to come down under a public order act for "causing harassment, alarm and distress."

SAXON SEDGEFORD (1998) —Life is peaceful in Sedgeford, not far inland from Hunstanton. But it wasn't always like that as villagers and a team of archaeologists have been finding out. In Saxon times, women suffered arthritis at the age of 20. Life was short with few people chalking up more than 45 years, according to an international team of researchers on an archaeological dig there.

Every summer for the last twenty-one years a team of volunteer archaeologists has gathered in the village of Sedgeford. Their work has centred on the Anglo-Saxon village where North Folk lived beside the river Heacham.

AUGUST

DISCOMFORTING ... (1984) – Now what are they up to in north Norfolk? Just sifting through bold new policies aimed at trying to attract more holidaymakers. One suggestion is that the district council might launch a promotional record "although this might not fit in with north Norfolk's image." What a revolting thought ..... "Viva Cromer!", "Shannock Rock" or "Runton Rave."

TWIN PEAKS (1985) – Identical twins Paul and Graham Fulcher chalk up identical standards of academic excellence. The 17-year-old brothers live at Ashill and have both been students at Hamond's Sixth Form Centre in Swaffham. They've just received outstanding A-level results in exactly the same subjects. They scoop the top A grade in mathematics, further mathematics, chemistry and physics. And both are awarded a distinction at Scholarship Level in maths. They're off to Churchill College at Cambridge – to read maths.

FORKING OUT (1986) – A pair of table forks fetch a remarkable £1,300 at an auction in Norwich The high price paid is due to their age and rarity. They were made in 1691. The auctioneer says: "People would have paid more had they been in better condition."

POLITICAL AIMS (1987) – Fakenham Bowmen's Club can't find volunteers to play the part of William Tell for their sponsored archery shoot – so they use pictures of politicians instead. They hold a sponsored apple shoot to buy equipment for youngsters wanting to join the club. They ask for volunteers to stand with apples on their heads. No takers – and so they use portraits of Margaret Thatcher and David Owen.

LOO AND BEHOLD! **(1988)** — Red faces in Norwich's Redwell Street as the city's first musical superloo is installed the wrong way round. The 10p-a-go loo could pave the way for five others if it proves a success. The city council will turn the loo, which features soothing "chamber music" and flushes automatically, the right way round before it is connected up.

LOST LAND (1989) — Gardener Bob Tubby wins an award for the best-kept allotment — but it's a hollow victory for the 66-year-old farm worker. Later this year Mr Tubby of Horsford will lose the land he and his father have tended for more than 70 years. The site is to be used for development.

RAPID DECLINE (1990) — Farming's full-time labour force continues to decline rapidly. More than 8,000 full-time jobs have been lost on the land in the past two years. Business links forged over decades will be broken when R.C. Edmondson shuts its agricultural marketing division at Fakenham in October.

BLESSED RUINS (1991) — Bride Ruth Murden is determined to have her marriage blessed at her village church — even though it was engulfed by the sea nearly 400 years ago. To the surprise of guests expecting to sit down to the wedding breakfast, she and new husband Robert Spruce walk over the sands to the ruins of St Mary's Church at Eccles-on-Sea, They are blessed by the Rev Albert Codman beside the remains minutes after he had performed the wedding ceremony in nearby Hempstead Church.

BENNETT BEAUTY (1992) — One of the best lines to savour for a long while in an Alan Bennett play on television. A woman with no sense of humour draws the gem: "She could only see a joke by appointment."

RESTORATION JOB (1993) — A three-month project to restore one of Norfolk's most treasured historic buildings begins at St Nicholas Church in Great Yarmouth. Crumbling pinnacles on the largest parish church in England are being refurbished in the latest stage of a rolling

St Nicholas Church, Great Yarmouth, much of which was rebuilt after wartime bombing but needing attention to the pinnacles in 1993.

restoration programme. Mortar between the Victorian pinnacles had deteriorated so badly that part of the churchyard had to be fenced off to protect passers-by from falling masonry.

CALENDAR SHOTS (1994) – I catch the bus from Cromer into Norwich as the rail strike continues. The journey takes a little longer but that's no hardship while the sun beats down on the picturesque route into Aylsham. Churches and cottages peer across meadows and cornfields ... classic calendar pictures of Norfolk serenity. I'm sorely tempted to get off the rapidly-filling bus and stroll into the countryside, perhaps arriving in Aylsham market place in time for lunch.

DARK PICKINGS (1995) – Organised gangs with a taste for strawberries are taking the invitation to "pick your own" a bit too literally. Crops worth thousands of pounds have been stolen in midnight raids on farms across Norfolk. Latest thefts come just weeks after rocketing potato prices led to raids on Norfolk fields — and even prompted some fish-and-chip shops to fit special alarms.

CATHEDRAL RUMPUS (1996) — Fury erupts in the hallowed cloisters of Norwich Cathedral as hundreds of ticket-holders are turned away from an open-air celebration of the building's 900th anniversary. Some 500 people who had bought tickets in advance for the first night of Fire from Heaven, staged by the Theatre Royal, are barred from raised seating in the cloisters. Furious Theatre Royal officials blame a last-minute decision by Norwich City Council for restricting the number of people allowed on the scaffold seating. Police are called as tempers boil over.

FOWL PLAY (1997) — Madcap comic Freddie Starr is branded "cruel" and "wicked" after flinging live chickens into the audience during a Yarmouth show. There are loud screams and some patrons try to throw the birds back onto stage after the comedian pulls the chickens from a fake body on an operating table as part of the sketch. But the prank misfires when appalled theatre-goers march out in protest at the Britannia.

HALL HAT-TRICK (1998) — One of the proudest days of my life in the public eye as I open the new village hall in my home patch of Beeston. And it is a grand session for community life in other parts of the county. David Wheeler, of the Norfolk Rural Community Council, opens a new hall at Wood Norton. Broadcaster John Timpson does the honours at a new £160,000 building at Toftwood. Big rays of sunshine on a rain-lashed Saturday.

TIGHT LEASH (1998) — Family outing to Norfolk's Rural Life Museum at Gressenhall. We enjoy a picnic before a stroll round Union Farm opposite. Children here on a tight leash mock my harvest holiday memories when we had freedom to explore hedgerow and headland, field and farm. I also suffer twinges of unease sizing up farming displays in the old workhouse. Some of these exhibits were part of the farming world of my boyhood. All of a sudden, that world is in a museum!

POSTAL PERILS (1999) — Two neighbours find they have something in common when they move into their new homes — the same name. Michael Wood comes face-to-face with his namesake as they empty removal vans on a development at Thorpe Marriott, on the outskirts of Norwich. To make matters worse for the postman, one calls his home Rosewood and the other Oakwood. To prevent even more confusion, they decide to use their initials on letters to distinguish them — one being Michael A Wood and the other Michael W Wood.

SILLY SEASON (2000) — When Malcolm and June Purvis tie the knot, their biggest decision isn't about the car, the cake or the venue. It is who will be the back-end and who will be up front. The couple from Palgrave, near Diss, reduce unsuspecting guests to hysterics by getting married as a pantomime camel after visiting a fancy dress shop in Norwich. June takes the back-end role.

RARE VISITOR (2001) — A bevy of insect "twitchers" descend on a Norfolk pond to watch a rare newcomer to the county. A squadron of small red-eyed damselflies is the focus of attention through a battery of binoculars. It's thought to be the first time the migrant dragonfly has been spotted in Norfolk. A wildlife watchers' jungle telegraph is hard at work to bring a string of enthusiasts to the roadside pond at Felbrigg, not far from Cromer.

POSH NOSH (2002) — East Anglia is top spot for online grocery shopping, thanks to lavish orders of well-heeled Londoners with second homes. Supermarkets report a huge surge in the number of customers with posh capital addresses ordering fine food for their weekend retreats in upmarket parts of Norfolk and Suffolk. Salmon and champagne regularly top the posh nosh shopping lists which sometimes add up to more than £1,000. So much for all that chat about wealthy visitors being good for our local stores!

CUP OVERFLOWS (2003) — Great Yarmouth Town Football Club has been picked to kick off the oldest and most famous football competition in the world from its modest Wellesley Road ground. The FA has brought forward the start of the first tie between the Bloaters and

West London outfit Southall to allow television cameras to broadcast the symbolic game.

BARROW BRIDE (2005) — It's hardly the most practical form of wedding transport. But a family joke turns to reality today as a blushing bride arrives at church in a modified builder's wheelbarrow. Karen Rumsby, 27, was eight years old when her father Roger joked he would wheel his daughter the short distance from their home to Tuttington Church on her wedding day. Father and bride turn a few heads as they arrive in style.

STAYING POWER (2006) — Ted Geeson's lawnmower sliced its first blade of grass in the year Queen Mary returned to Sandringham for the first time after King George V's death and the world caught its first glimpse of Hitler's Germany at the Berlin Olympics. Seven decades later, Ted is still whirling around his garden at Scarning, near East Dereham, proving that back then things really were built to last.

LICENSED TO SHRILL (2007) — Six little piggies from Binham have to jump through more than a few bureaucratic hoops to get on their way to the village fayre. The piglets are vital ingredients for the ancient game of guess-the-weight-of-the-pigs at Binham's medieval fayre. But, in order for them to make the 800-yard journey from Abbey Farm Piggery to stardom, owner Andrew Chubbock has to apply for a performing animal licence from the Animal Health Agency. He also has to obtain a licence from Trading Standards — and each piglet is given a tag with an identification number.

LOTS OF LADYBIRDS (2009) — This will go down as the Year of the Bishy-Barney-Bee Blitz on the north Norfolk coast. Hordes of ladybirds continue to congregate, especially along the seafront in Cromer, to provide an instant talking-point for visitors and locals alike. They are more of an irritant than a hazard but the novelty has worn off. I take latest news to Radio Norfolk in Norwich on my monthly mission to the studio. Even more ladybirds waiting to welcome me back.

PUSSY PRATTLE (2010) — Another bizarre mobile phone incident to add to my pile in evidence against them flagrantly upsetting the public. A woman in the bank is making a real hash of inserting her card and sorting out details for the assistant. Then the customer stops to take a call and very loudly makes arrangements for her two cats to be taken "into care" later in the month! She displays no embarrassment at all in regaling us with her pussy programme. I am amazed – and sorry – that the woman trying to look after her financial matters does not object. I mutter all the way down a crowded street about such shameless behaviour. Verging on the catastrophic …

FRINGE FUN (2011) – I am impressed by the Best Joke Awards at the Edinburgh Fringe Festival. First spot goes to: "I needed a password eight characters long, so I picked Snow White and the Seven Dwarfs." Runner-up is nearly as good: "Crime in multi-storey car parks. That is wrong on so many different levels."

DUZZY RASKEL (2012) – One of the most unlikely adventures of my creative career, filming at various locations across the county for a video to promote Police and Crime Commissioner elections in November. I

Duzzy Raskel on the road to stardom in a video to draw attention to the Police and Crime Commissioner elections.

have composed and recorded a sort of Norfolk rap to arouse interest in the local cause. With dark glasses and a baseball cap jutting sidewards, I ply my musical trade as Duzzy Raskel. It is hard work and very different to any of my other exploits.

WINDING DOWN (2013) — Breath of autumn in the air on the last day of a month carrying plenty of warm sunshine. I feel my usual cheerful self as September beckons with mellow days and cooler nights. Crammed Cromer can now shed a few stone and prove far more homely as the season winds down. I have chatted with more people than ever before who make it plain they prefer the town out of season. It seems it may no longer be heresy to say so.

LIMPENHOE SIX (2014) — Story of the six who went to fight in the First World War but never returned to their small Norfolk village is remembered during a poignant service. Residents gather at Limpenhoe, on the edge of the Broads and three miles from Reedham, to hear about the lives of the six — one of whom was just 15 when he died — as they gather for a special ceremony to rededicate the village war memorial. It has been given an overhaul to mark the centenary of the conflict.

VOWS RENEWED (2015) — We pick blackberries from our little jungle we call the back garden to make a crumble for Sunday tea. Plenty more on the way for the second successive year. I recently renewed my rural vows with a barefoot stroll across the corner of a freshly-harvested field the other side of Hanworth: "Stubble, stubble ... keep out trouble!"

SEPTEMBER

ROLLING HOME (1986) — Bringing home the harvest takes on a different meaning for regulars at the Woodfarm Inn, Wayford Bridge, near Stalham. Teams from all over Norfolk take part in the Giant Straw Bale Rolling Contest. The 19 four-man teams have to negotiate a series of obstacles during the event, which raises around £200 for the Norfolk Deaf Children's Association.

CASTLE NICKED! (1987) — Parish councillors at Old Buckenham are up in arms because New Buckenham has been given its historic castle by mistake on the village's heritage map. The error has been pointed out by Breckland District Council's senior planning officer for conservation. Now members are considering taking down the four maps mounted on display boards because the information is incorrect.

SIGNING UP (1988) — The parish of Langley with Hardley has at last been provided with its own village sign. The double-sided sign, close to the boundary of the two communities, is unveiled by the oldest resident from each village. The ceremony ends a ten-year wait since the idea was first mooted.

POINT OF VIEW (1988) — I'm invited to take part in a debate about the countryside in "Anglia Live" from the Norwich studios. A good idea — but the demands of instant "entertainment" offer few chances to pursue important strands in many arguments. For instance, a farmer says pulling up the hedgerows affords much better views!

AMY'S BIG DAY (1989) — Cheering villagers line the pavements to sing "Happy Birthday!" to their favourite great-great-grandmother, 100-year-old Amy Morton. The sprightly centenarian makes a right royal tour of Great Hockham, eight miles from Thetford, in a horse-drawn wagonette. Locals offer flowers, cards, gifts and songs as Amy is driven to a party with five generations of her own family.

DISMAL DISHES (1990) — Councillor Jocelyn Rawlence coins a new expression during a debate on satellite dishes. "Hideosities" is how she describes the white discs sprouting on house fronts around south Norfolk. "The commercial side is going ahead willy-nilly and they didn't realise the impact it was going to have on the countryside" she tells South Norfolk planning committee.

GOING DUTCH (1990) — Eels poached from Norfolk rivers are ending up on the tables of rich Dutch families. Poachers steal along the river banks of Norfolk and Suffolk in the dead of night to catch the highly-prized delicacy which the Dutch consume in vast quantities. They pay up to £10 a pound for the privilege.

SHATTERED MYTH (1992) — The "myth of idyllic country life" is shattered by a report which reveals the extent of poverty, suicide and deprivation in Britain's villages. The study comes from an influential body of businessmen and experts headed by the country's richest man, the Duke of Westminster. He says: "People in the countryside may not be rioting but they do more serious things like killing themselves, They are doing it quietly and it does not make the headlines."

ALMIGHTY SNARL (1992) – Latest reported sighting of a mystery wildcat in rural Norfolk. Housewife Rosemary Blanch of Tunstead says: "I heard about the wildcat and didn't believe it. Then last night I heard an almighty snarl and today I saw the cat in the fields. It didn't look friendly."

WINDOW JOYS (1993) — Darkness at noon as rain lashes down to mock all my salutes to a favourite month. Weather still on the move as I catch my train home from Norwich to Cromer. Sun glints on a church spire, the moment thrown into sharp and exciting focus by heavy skies. A kaleidoscope of scenery through the train window brings much pleasure and I await the autumn fashion show with more interest than usual.

WILDLIFE BOOST (1994) — Good to look at the other side of the coin now and again. A conservation area created following the excavation of 500,000 tonnes of sand and gravel from Norfolk farmland is officially opened. Creaking Gate Lake at Bittering, next door to my home village of Beeston, was a quarry worked by Tarmac Roadstone. Now, as part of the original planning permission, Tarmac has created a picturesque landscape teeming with wildlife.

REARING FIRST (1995) — Charles William Green, the first farmer in Norfolk to rear a cow through artificial insemination, dies at 98. Born at the Black Horse pub in Castle Rising in 1897, he moved to Walnut Tree Farm at Norton Subcourse in 1913 and farmed there for more than half-a-century.

TRUNCH TREAT (1996) — Happy evening at Trunch Village hall for the locals' harvest supper. I have to sing for mine — but it's a warm and receptive climate. I sit next to "Mr Trunch", Arthur Amis, born in the village in 1907 and author of the delightful memoirs, From Dawn to Dusk. He recalls the hall being built in 1912 "for just under £500." They've already named a road after him in the village, Amis Close, and two newcomers from Buckinghamshire sitting opposite live there. We joke about landlord Arthur and his clients — and they say they're reading his book to find out more about their new home.

TED TO RESCUE (1997) — Ted Woods responds to Norfolk's chronic shortage of soccer referees by signing up at 77. The veteran with a fitness programme that would put men half his age to shame comes out of retirement to referee up to three matches a week as a Norfolk County FA- approved official. Ted, who refereed into his early 70s until a hernia operation ended his long career, returns to action in two Crusader Sunday League friendlies.

Trunch stalwart Arthur Amis and friend. They named a road after Arthur in the village while he was still alive!

REMOTE VOICE (1999) — A Norfolk councillor living 230 miles from residents she's supposed to be representing decides to resign. Broadland Labour councillor Elizabeth Dilworth "temporarily moved" to the Lake District in March. Six months later, she had not returned and residents in her Great Witchingham ward were becoming irritated. Villagers wanted to turn to Mrs Dilworth to complain about a terrible smell in the village. Now she writes: "I am fully prepared to admit that my efforts have not improved matters and in view of my continued absence from the area I have resigned." A by-election will be held in November.

LORDLY LIFT (2000) — Now, this is stylish living! Lord Robin Walpole collects me from Cromer to attend the Itteringham harvest supper in the village hall — and returns me safely before midnight. He's always amiable company. A glorious sunset marks our journey to one of the most alluring parts of the area. White owls swoop as the light fades. We chat about the environment, one of his main passions, the way Norfolk is changing and how some aspects remain strong and true.

AUTUMN'S BREATH (2002) — I feel the first breath of autumn on my cheeks as I sit outside to soak up the clear glories of September's first day. Same soothing effect as I walk round the block and down to the seafront. Yes, a definite tinge on the breeze as if to salute the impending change of seasons. I can hear whispers as the trees are ruffled. They're not warnings, more like little promises of cheering days to come before winter's onset.

THE PAGE TURNS (2003) — A village which took on the might of Norfolk County Council celebrates success as it hails the reopening of its local library. Bradwell refused to accept defeat when the county council closed the library in a cost-cutting exercise and mounted a community DIY campaign. The Books for Bradwell appeal says 15,000 books have been donated, allowing the library to reopen next month.

RURAL HAVENS (2004) — Always a relief to discover — and revisit — havens of peace in rural areas of the county. I need constant reassurance that these spots are there and comparatively safe. A blackberry-picking expedition takes us down a leafy lane towards Hanworth, just a few miles from Cromer's bustle. Only a few September days left as we accept it's hardly a vintage season for hedgerow bounty. Still, the setting is so rewarding with wide open acres between church and Hanworth Hall. A pheasant rises noisily as if to warn us not to loiter on his domain.

DOGGED BY NOISES (2005) — Emphatic proof that Swaffham is going to the dogs! I'm in town for a chat to the Wissey Group of Women's Institutes in the Church Rooms. I have serious competition. A dogs' obedience class is being held in the room above and there are several "paws" in proceedings for barks, scratches and squeals. I make use of the interruptions to make bad jokes about a Norfolk version of Crufts, a Spaniel in the works and Black Shuck moving inland.

RICH HARVEST (2007) — A remarkable witness to more than a century of dramatic changes to Norfolk farming and the countryside has ploughed his final furrow. Hedley Thurtle, hailed as the oldest farmer in Britain, took part in 97 consecutive harvests. He dies at 102 at his farm in Bodham, near Holt. He was still helping with the harvest, carting grain with a tractor and trailer, until daughter Elizabeth persuaded him to give up driving just five years ago.

OAR-INSPIRING (2009) — A Broadland vicar makes the most of the riverside setting of his parishes as he rows 15 miles between villages to raise money for the upkeep of his churches. The Rev Neville Khambatta rows himself around Ludham, Catfield, Hickling and Potter Heigham to prove his theory that he's the only vicar in England who can travel around his whole benefice by water.

DASHING DAVE (2010) — A man from Southery, seven miles from Downham Market, raises almost £2,500 for a cancer charity by circumnavigating Norfolk on a moped. Dave Fletcher, known affectionately as the "Fat Bloke on a Moped", completes the 188-mile route in seven hours and 20 minutes at an average speed of 25 mph.

WOOLLY JUMPERS (2011) — A thoroughbred line-up ensures punters are not fleeced at a jump racing meeting with a difference —

the Beachamwell Lamb National. Visitors flock to watch the second annual sheep steeplechase at the village fete and country fair. Some leave counting their winnings after a £1 flutter on the fluffy racers with names such as Sherbaa, Lady Baa Baa and Rambo. But the victor in the first dramatic encounter of the day is Ewesain Bolt, emulating the record-breaking heroics of its sprinting namesake in the 100m relay at the World Athletics Championships on the same afternoon.

SCHOOL EXTRAS (2012) — Children at a Norfolk primary school will enjoy lessons with a difference after the installation of three new wind turbines. They've been named Tom, Dick and Harry. These small-scale additions at Swanton Morley will become part of the curriculum across different subjects in addition to helping cut the school's energy bills.

DIFFERENT TRACKS (2013) — I board a packed train from Cromer to Norwich, many of the passengers on the last laps of their summer holidays. Such contrasts to notice along the way. A young mother with three youngsters trying to demand attention spends most of the journey making small talk on her mobile phone. A Norfolk grandmother chats cheerfully and informatively to her little grandson, endearing him to all nearby by calling him "a barrow-load of monkeys!"

LONGEST STRIKE (2014) — A small south Norfolk village is awash with union flags as over 1,000 people gather to mark the 100th anniversary of the start of the longest strike in English history. The rural drama was sparked by children at Burston School after their teachers, Tom and Kitty Higdon, were dismissed. It lasted from April, 1914 until just before the Second World War. Socialist leaders and trade unionists from across the country became involved. The Strike School is now a museum.

TRUE ROMANCE (2014) — A simple Norfolk love story pulls on heartstrings all over the world. Gordon Olley surprises his wife Mary by re-enacting their first date 50 years ago. He not only arranges for them to see the same film but also hires out the same venue — Dereham cinema. Their story makes national and international headlines, with a Hong Kong website even creating an animation of the lovebirds.

PAIR OF ACES (2015) — The odds are a staggering 25 million to one — but two Norfolk golfers playing against each other can reflect on a remarkable few minutes in which thy both sank a hole-in-one at the same hole. In memorable scenes at the Royal Norwich Golf Club in Hellesdon — soon to be covered by houses if developers get their way — Aaron Saddleton and Mark Avis land aces on the course's par-three ninth hole.

SOUL-LIFTING (2015) — A shaft of evening sunlight across part of a fresh field of corn stubble on the outskirts of Flordon lifts the soul after weeks of reading about even more development plans for precious bits of rural Norfolk. Our final Mardling and Music Evening of the season takes us beyond Swardeston, Mulbarton and Bracon Ash to the small village of Flordon and St Michael's Church on a site below houses and a rutted lane. This ancient building also serves as the community centre and there's a compelling country feel for our well-attended finale.

The Burston Strike School continues to be a symbolic meeting place each September, to remember the stand taken by Tom and Kitty Higdon.

OCTOBER

KEEPING WATCH (1985) — Good to know Broadland District Council will keep a close watch on progress of the Horsford, Drayton and Taverham growth area to "ensure a balanced development". Let's hope we don't have cause to dub it "The Infernal Triangle." Norwich suburban sprawl seems set to continue whatever honeyed words come from council chambers. I fear there'll be much to regret in a decade or so. If not before.

SWALLOW THAT! (1985) — End of the line for George Latimer Williams after 21 years as Clerk to the Justices of Norwich magistrates' Court. He's seen the move from the Guildhall to Bishopgate completed. His favourite memory is of a defendant eating an outdated vehicle tax disc and then expecting the magistrates to swallow the story of his innocence. They didn't.

WHAT'S IN A NAME? (1988) — The name Hooker Close, suggested by a Norfolk clergyman for a new housing estate near his church, is thrown out following objections from people considering buying properties there. Councillors in west Norfolk approve Cuthbert Close as a suitable alternative. The Rural Dean of Lynn, Canon Maurice Green, says when he submitted the name he was ignorant of its association with women of ill repute. He explains that Richard Hooker was a 16th century notable at the time of the Reformation and a great Christian theologian. Roads on the new development around All Saints' Church, North Wootton, have been named after Christian saints and leading theologians.

LIGHTING UP (1989) — Can this be true? A gang of willing workers putting up the Christmas lights in Cromer on a wonderfully bright Sunday morning in mid-October! While one can admire the enthusiasm and community spirit behind this operation, it's sad to think it is necessary a fortnight before the clock go back. I object each year to the indecent haste with which we pave the way towards a wonderful festive season in the blatant name of commercialism.

MARCUS MAGIC (1990) — It's a case of "soft drinks all round" in the clubhouse after Eaton Golf Club junior member Marcus Barrett, aged 12, scores a hole-in-one. Marcus is on half-term holiday playing with friends when he achieves his ace at the 140-yard second hole. "I normally land in the bunker there" he says modestly.

TON-UP DINNER (1991) — Wind and rain provide a stormy cocktail for Cromer Cricket Club's centenary dinner. I propose a toast to the club with former captain Phil Mindham — a fellow old boy of Hamond's Grammar School at Swaffham — replying. I look back at what else was happening in 1891, from a horse with bad legs winning the Grand National to controversy caused at Cromer by men seen near the "women's portion" of the bathing machines.

WELCOME CALL (1992) — A dramatic and welcome breakthrough! I have a call from Granada Television to help with a script for a programme featuring Norfolk characters. I am pleased to tell them the difference between the way we talk and our friends in the West Country. Indeed, this might spell the beginning of the end for the dastardly "Mummerzet" sound to which we have been subjected so often in national productions on radio and television.

WAY OF LIFE (1992) — One of those infuriatingly broad surveys suggests Norfolk is the most unfriendly place in the United Kingdom! And we're also said to have the most unwelcoming village in the nation — poor old Mileham, just a couple of miles from my old home patch of Beeston. The survey by Country Life Magazine reckons Norfolk villages are so proud of their roots they often jealously guard their way of life against newcomers. Quite right, too. Many of those also confuse justifiable caution with deliberate coldness.

HER AND HYMNS (1994) — Kathleen Brooks has been pulling out the stops for births, marriages and deaths of generations of Hickling families. Now the 83-year-old, organist at St Mary's Church for 56 years, plays her final hymn. She's rarely missed a Sunday over those years and has been part of so many christenings, weddings and funerals that she has lost count. "One of my special memories is of when I was asked to play for three weddings of three generations of the same family." A lovely village innings.

APPLE CAUSE (1995) — A memorable day bathed in autumn sunshine. I'm invited to open the apple orchard at the Norfolk Rural Life Museum in Gressenhall amid countless mardles and happy little reunions with folk from all over the county. Apples all the way and queues to have fruit identified are considerable. "Norfolk country life to the core!" exclaims one enthusiast.

TUNSTEAD TROSH (1996) — Mellow sun to bless the Tunstead Trosh, a celebration of farming's good old days with horses and threshing tackle to the fore. I "open" the event at 2pm although there's been plenty going on throughout the morning. A Suffolk exhibitor says they had found Tunstead on the map but were still looking for Tunstead Trosh. We may well chuckle — but anyone could make a mistake like that.

CHARMING CHEQUERS (1997) — Time stands still at the Chequers pub in Gresham, a few miles from Cromer. Landlady Winnie Lawes admits little has changed in the half-century she's been running it. Apart from moving the toilets indoors and knocking the main bar through into the snug, it has barely altered since she took over in October, 1947. Winnie fights shy of food, music and modernisation "because the locals like it this way."

THE LAST POST (1998) — Hilda White's rural post office at Saxthorpe, six miles from Aylsham, has changed very little since she took it over

A song of praise for farming's old way at the Tunstead Trosh. In times past,
Captain Swing and the wreckers broke farm machinery when it was introduced;
now we are devoted to keeping it running.

from her grandfather in 1942. She started using an electronic calculator two weeks ago. Now the prospect of joining the computer age leads 82-year-old Hilda to retire. "I have been here since I was six months old and all this talk of computers has made me ill" she says. Generations have passed through her doors and she's had only two days off in 56 years – one to go to a royal garden party.

FOND FORMED (1999) – Friends Of Norfolk Dialect officially launched at Yaxham Village Hall – and I'm asked to fill the post of chairman. I accept with a deal of pride and optimism It's a day I hope future generations will salute with gratitude. Over 40 enthusiasts present and I know we have wide support, not least from Norfolk exiles.

FAREWELL GEORGE (2000) – George Jessup's funeral at Watton parish church. I am invited to share a few reflections. George, 88, wrote widely about his beloved Breckland for half-a-century, gave illustrated talks, led fascinating walks and raised thousands of pounds for charity. Our lads have been helping grandad in the garden at Drayton and are in their rough outdoor clothes when we return to collect them. "A perfect summary of our day" I say to Diane. "Three Weedings and a Funeral!"". George would have liked that.

SO EVOCATIVE (2001) – To Norwich by train to give a talk to the Norfolk Cricket Society. Arriving early, I take a stroll as light fades and find a near-mystical experience crunching over crisp autumn leaves along the cobbles of Elm Hill. I guess who and what might be behind shuttered windows as I wander through one of the city's most atmospheric spots. Street lights pour down reassurance not far from what turns into a frenzy of late-night life on Tombland.

CLOCK MISERY (2003) – A Norfolk vicar called Bell is involved in a right old ding-dong over the chimes of his church clock. A couple living in the shadow of Fakenham parish church claim their lives are being made a misery by the noise of the Westminster chimes from the rare and recently-restored clock. The vicar, the Rev Andrew Bell, says that while he sympathises, the chimes are popular with townsfolk and there's nothing he can do to make them quieter.

LUCKY ESCAPE (2004) – A devoted widower falls over a clifftop as he plants daffodil bulbs in memory of his wife. The tumble by an 84-year-old Welshman sparks a rescue operation involving two helicopters, coastguards, ambulance, fire crews and police. Remarkably, he escapes with hardly a scratch as bushes on the cliffs at Beeston Bump break his fall.

RIGHT TO ROAM (2005) – Ramblers and walkers put their best feet forward to celebrate the new "right to roam" over thousands of acres across Norfolk and Suffolk. After more than a century of campaigning, 22,000 acres of land in Norfolk and 12,000 in Suffolk are now fully open to the public for the first time. The move comes as part of a nationwide review of the countryside and terms of the Countryside and Rights of Way Act, 2000.

RESTORING FAITH (2007) – A pensioner who suffered a harrowing robbery speaks of how a touching gesture by schoolchildren has restored some of her faith in human nature. Children at a primary school in Northwold, near Brandon, raise £380 for the partially-sighted 83-year-old who was threatened and held down by raiders in her own home. "I feel very touched and very pleased at what they did" she says of the local pupils.

END OF ERA (2008) – Clocks go back an hour as we reflect on 25 years of local entertainment. The curtain falls on Press Gang adventures on Cromer pier in the Pavilion Theatre where it all started in the summer of 1984. Sell-out houses for afternoon and evening shows make it a successful and emotional farewell. Old friend Sid Kipper, Norfolk's main cultural ambassador, is our celebrated warm-up man.

BILLY'S RETURN (2009) – He was forced to leave his ancestral home along with his family and nearly 1,000 others at the height of the Second World War. But a Breckland man's final wishes are fulfilled as he's buried in the churchyard of the village where he was born. All military activity in the Thetford Battle Area is suspended for several hours as Billy Hancock, 85, is interred at the parish church in the deserted village of Tottington. He's the first person to be laid to rest in the churchyard for more than half-a-century after villagers from Tottington and several other nearby communities, were evicted from their homes in 1942 for the 17,500-acre military training area. Promises made that they would be allowed to return after the war were never fulfilled. Billy Hancock was an ardent campaigner for people to be allowed more access to their former homes and to return to them for good.

PICA IS HOME (2010) — An Anglo-Saxon warrior makes a triumphant return to his Norfolk home in a stunning life-size sculpture. When the traditional village sign started to turn scruffy, the parish council in North Pickenham, near Swaffham, commissioned local sculptor Colin Yorke to create an unusual replacement. Using a single piece of locally-sourced elm, the figure of Anglo-Saxon leader Pica is carved. He gave his name to the village.

REVVING REV (2011) — A new vicar starts his job at full throttle — astride an Enfield Bullet 350cc motorbike. The Rev John Stride, 63, raises a few eyebrows while spotted travelling around his new circuit comprising Ludham, Hickling, Catfield and Potter Heigham on two wheels. Isn't there something in the Bible about "David's Triumph" heard throughout Israel?

MILESTONE MAGIC (2012) — Memorable night on Cromer Pier to mark my 50 years as Norfolk scribe and mardler. A full house in the Pavilion Theatre despite wind and rain as Radio Norfolk's zany panel game Should The Team Think? is brought out of retirement for the occasion. The Bishop of Norwich, the Rt Rev Graham James — currently the subject of intense speculation about the next Archbishop of Canterbury — partners me against television's Carol Bundock and Cromer favourite Olly Day. David Clayton in the chair as usual while former Radio Norfolk colleague Tony Mallion also returns as producer. At the end of the show, the new Eastern Daily Press editor Nigel Pickover mounts the stage to present me with a mock-up front page headlined "Legend Keith" and a bottle of champagne.

PAVILION END (2013) — Lakenham's thatched cricket pavilion is to be knocked down amid cries of "vandalism! " across Norfolk and beyond. A planning inspector rules local councillors were wrong to block its demolition. Norwich City Council's planning committee decided in February to turn down plans for the old cricket ground in the heart of the city, formerly the home of Norfolk cricket. The developers appealed — and a planning officer now allows that appeal, so granting outline permission to build 75 houses on the land. "I find there is very little significance in the pavilion or its setting" says inspector Tim Wood. I lived next door to the cricket ground for over a decade and grew to love that pavilion.

LATE TREAT (2014) — Over 200 people tuck into the turkey dinners they were supposed to have enjoyed last Christmas. Flood victims from Norfolk coastal villages Walcott and Bacton are joined for the meal at Walcott's Lighthouse Inn by dozens who helped them after last December's devastating tidal surge. For many it is a first return to the Lighthouse since that fateful night when the pub was used as an evacuation centre.

FISH MARATHON (2015) — Colin and Valerie Earl retire after selling fish from a pitch on Fakenham Market since 1954. "It's a sad day" sighs 82-year-old Colin. "I should have had another year but I was getting pressure from the wife. She says she can't stand another winter out here. Then she got back-up from our daughters. We've got four of them, so you can tell the flak I was under". The couple from Foulsham also sold fish door-to-door in the villages. Colin is not sure what he'll do on Thursdays from next week. "I'm going to learn to do the hoovering" he jokes.

EGGS AND BRACES (2015) – Cromer is pulling on its autumn shawl. I sense it's all a bit slower today on the outdoor market and there's less bustle along Garden Street. I resume my hunt for a new pair of braces. I strike lucky and return home with them and a dozen extra-large eggs purchased on the market. Sometimes my penchant for variety takes some beating.

NOVEMBER

FREE ADVERTS (1985) — A fleeting television appearance during the annual *Children in Need* marathon. I represent BBC Radio Norfolk in the local studios over the road on All Saints Green. I can't call it either an entertaining or edifying experience. The frantic drive for money, desperately needed though it may be, is turning into a massive excuse to provide free advertising for business interests which see it as the ideal vehicle for such a purpose.

TREASURE HUNT (1987) — History lessons at Methwold High School take on a whole new meaning after the discovery of Roman ruins close to the school playing-fields. Lessons are no longer restricted to classrooms for second-year pupils. They are spent trudging through a neighbouring cornfield in the hope of uncovering Roman treasures. The site was a Roman villa or farm and youngsters have found tiles, several in excellent condition, used in floors as well as roofs.

BETTER LATE ... (1988) — Cromer town councillors appreciate one good turn deserves another — even if takes almost 250 years! They agree to give £10 towards a restoration appeal for a Cambridgeshire village church because parishioners there helped Cromer fire victims in 1740. Church wardens at St Peter's, Wentworth, near Ely, write to Cromer Town Council saying their village, with a population of 120, needs urgent financial support towards re-roofing. Checking through old church records for February, 1740, they found the entry: "Collected then at Wentworth for the sufferers by fire at the town of Cromer in the County of Norfolk, the sum of one shilling and sixpence."

GRATEFUL COX (1989) — A lifeboat coxswain praises his own crew for rescuing him during a fishing trip. Benny Read, cox of the independent

Caister lifeboat, gets into trouble when his fishing vessel is caught in a heavy swell with an extra-large haul and is about to flounder. Without the Caister crew's help he and two other men "would have gone down like a bit of lead." Mr Read's boat, The Comet, is escorted to Caister and beached after transferring part of his haul. "It's what the lifeboat is there for" says a relieved Caister cox.

HOLDING ON (1989) – I visit the Ludham Society for a mardle. I voice deep fears for the county I love and then ask for questions from the audience. One woman, a newcomer to the area, asks what it is I am desperate to hold on to .... My considered response is "the sense of local pride, identity and community as reflected in the village life of my youth."

ON WAY OUT – (1990) – There are still more than 60 schools in Norfolk with outside toilets. They could soon be consigned to history. New Education Secretary Kenneth Clarke announces an extra £600m will be spent on school buildings from next April. That extra money was won in the battle with other government departments when South Norfolk MP John MacGregor was Leader of the House.

OVER A TON (1990) – Ann Scott of Wymondham runs a competition at her local Women's Institute to guess how many gallstones she had removed in a recent operation. She raises £11 for Children in Need. The correct total is 106.

DIRTY PLAYER (1991) – "Midfielder needed service of a sweeper" says a clever Eastern Daily Press headline as Norwich City footballer Tim Sherwood is fined £50 and ordered to pay £25 costs for dumping broken bottles, rubbish bags and parts of an old sink beside a country road. He pleads guilty to dropping litter in a public place.

REGAL SALUTE (1992) – The Queen reveals Norfolk is her favourite county as she meets a party of local schoolchildren. Speaking to pupils from Dereham Neatherd High School as they receive a national award for environment work, she asks if they are from Dereham in Norfolk. On learning that they are, she says she's delighted as it is her favourite place, especially with Sandringham being there.

Jim Smellie – with the name for the job

NAME FOR THE JOB (1992) – Death of Jim Smellie, the Norfolk public health officer who gained national acclaim for having such an apt name for the job. A native of Lancashire, he won recognition in the national press, in Punch and on Esther Rantzen's *That's Life* television show because of his name. He moved to East Anglia in 1949 and became chief public health officer for Norwich in 1960. On retirement he went into partnership with son Richard – raising pigs in Costessey.

SEAFRONT DRAMA (1993) – Cromer Pier is sliced in two by a runaway rig on a stormy Sunday! The end-of-the-pier theatre and lifeboat shed are marooned at sea. We learn later that a Bailey bridge will be slung across the gap to allow lifeboatmen to reach their craft. North Norfolk District Council chief executive Terry Nolan pledges the pier will be fully restored in time for the next summer season. Real incentive to get a move on!

SEAGULL SALUTE (1994) – Church bells toll across town at the start of Remembrance Sunday. My solo stroll is marked by a stunning flypast of seagulls soaring and scattering and skimming above the gravestones as the peals pause before 11 am. I move on to the seafront to pay my respects alongside Henry Blogg as his bronze head looks at the waves and seems to nod gently at all the memories riding on them.

SHATTERED PEACE (1995) – Why does it take an "important" report from a major organisation to make us aware of the startlingly obvious? The Campaign for the Protection of Rural England tells us the peace of large parts of this region have been shattered in the past 30 years by development, new roads and increasing traffic. It points out that since the 1960s, a quiet area more than 25 times the size of Norwich has been lost, with rural Norfolk particularly at risk. Yes, I have noticed odd signs of the old place going downhill on my rounds ...

SPECIAL GUEST (1997) – Winifred Brown goes back to the classroom and recalls her schooldays at Carleton Rode more than 80 years ago. The 92-year-old is special guest at what is thought to be Norfolk's oldest village primary school celebrating its 175th anniversary with the official opening of a new extension. She's joined by her great-great-grandson Lewis, a seven-year-old pupil at the school, to help with burying a time capsule by South Norfolk MP John MacGregor.

BELATED TRIBUTE (1998) – He could not be honoured by having his name associated with a new housing development. But villagers at Beetley can now pay tribute to long-serving Labour councillor Bryan Barnard with the opening of a play area bearing his name. A long-running dispute erupted two years ago when residents of luxury homes who had moved in from London claimed the name of a Socialist politician linked to their development would give the wrong impression and could reduce property values. The row ended in court with magistrates ruling Mr Barnard's name should not be used and a compromise reached. Now villagers honour him with a plaque at the new Bryan Barnard Children's Playground, part of the Beetley River Meadows Scheme.

SWITCHING ON (1999) – It's been stuck in the dark ages for far too long but a Norfolk church is now switching on to the 20th century ... just in time for the 21st. The medieval church at Mautby, near Yarmouth, has been cold and damp for longer than most and the hardy congregation would sometimes endure near-freezing temperatures. Now light and heat extinguish the need for candles in the 12th century church of St Peter & St Paul.

USEFUL PUSH (2001) – Norfolk villagers receive royal encouragement to tackle the county's rural housing problem. Spiralling house prices, low wages and the sale of council houses are among factors forcing many working folk out of their native villages. The Princess Royal, president of the Rural Housing Trust, joins the charity at a seminar in Hempnall to explain to parish councils how they can promote and develop affordable housing schemes.

HEAD SOUTH (2002) – Important message for women wishing to live to a ripe old age – move to South Norfolk, where life expectancy is among highest in the country. According to a new survey, women in South Norfolk can typically expect to live until 82.3 years of age. That's fourth highest out of 374 local authorities surveyed in England and Wales.

BLUE PLAQUE (2003) – Acting legend Sir Michael Caine returns to his Norfolk childhood – and tells of the feisty headmistress who taught him to play poker and smoke cigarettes. Sir Michael visits North Runcton, near King's Lynn, to unveil a blue plaque marking his time spent in the village as an evacuee during the Second World War.

FAMILY FURROWS (2004) – Four generations of a Norfolk farming family make history as a great-grandfather guides a single-furrowed plough. The 92-year-old retired farmer, Bert Bunting from Skeyton, ploughs with a pair of heavy horses alongside his son Colin, grandson Stewart and two great-grandsons, Scott and Rees.

POLICE ESCORT (2005) – Residents of a Thetford estate are greeted with an unusual sight when the lorries sent to collect their rubbish arrive with a police escort. Officers are called to the Abbey Estate after a householder swears at binmen over a dispute regarding a drive by Breckland Council to get people to put waste in the right bin.

HOLY ORDERS? (2006) – Bishop of Norwich, the Rt Rev Graham James, does the launching honours for my *Bumper Book of Norfolk Squit* in the third-floor restaurant at Jarrold's store in the city. There's loud laughter when the Bishop's humorous flow is broken by a tannoy announcement that the store is due to close in five minutes! Bishop Graham underlines the fact it's a woman's voice from above.

JEM'S CENTENARY (2010) – A pilgrimage to Beeston churchyard in my home village to mark the 100th anniversary of the death of Jem Mace, heavyweight boxing champion of the world. I travel with Julie Pinnington, Jem's great-great-grand-daughter and only known direct descendant living in Norfolk, and her husband John.

The Bishop of Norwich, the Rt Rev Graham James, gives his blessing to Skip's
'Bumper Book of Norfolk Squit'.

They live at Kelling, near Holt, and Julie has mixed feelings about her illustrious boxing ancestor. Jem was a serial philanderer and gambler who scandalised parts of Victorian society with his antics. His memorial in Beeston churchyard stands next to the grave of his father, William.

END OF LINE (2011) — The 10.45 from King's Cross arrives bang on time. Train driver Bernie Rolfe steps out of the cab for the last time after 50 years on the railways. A buffer of balloons and posters is waiting to welcome Bernie as he pulls into King's Lynn station. Friends and colleagues are on the platform to greet him. Bernie started his career in days of steam at the March station.

FLOOD HERO (2012) — A hero who saved more than 20 lives when the 1953 floods ravaged the Norfolk coastline dies at 81 at his home in America. But his memory immediately lives on as US servicemen and women march through Hunstanton before a footpath is named after him. Reis Leming waded into icy water towing a rubber dinghy after angry waves broke through sea defences south of Hunstanton. Before he passed out from the cold, he plucked 27 people to safety.

TUNEFUL TWIST (2013) — Carol-singing campaigners show their opposition to proposed new homes in their village with a tuneful twist. Dressed in Victorian clothing to reflect Trowse's heritage, about 30 villagers sing specially-adapted carols on Trowse Common before moving into the city to perform outside The Forum. The group, under the banner of Keep Trowse Special, claim more new houses would change the village beyond comparison and betray its history as the UK's first model village. A bit early for carols — but it's never too soon to protest!

"CRESTA RUN" (2024) — Long trip to Belton for a chat with the local history society. Rain lashes down all the way there and back. The "Cresta Run" entry to Gorleston — high concrete walls either side with a whiff of doom about them — never fails to prompt an outburst of utter despair. Who on earth gave permission for this hideous excess? And some of the growing sprawl beyond Gorleston seems to be stamped with the same disregard for character. Road "improvements" with new housing estates sticking out at the sides merely add to a heart-rending scene. Even if more new homes are desperately needed, this is no place for them.

BATSON BOWS OUT (2015) — I join the throng in the Cromer press office as colleagues, friends and admirers wish Richard Batson well. He's moving on after 23 years in charge of the Cromer set-up and 40 years altogether in local newspapers. I've got to know him well as a top-rate Norfolk reporter and commentator always ready to chat and share a good pun however busy his schedule. Richard has used what are rapidly becoming old-fashioned virtues, like cheerfulness and careful listening, to keep his career going. He admits Cromer has been his favourite base.

MILESTONE MELODIES (2015) — Happy night on Cromer Pier with Sheringham Shantymen for the last of their 25th anniversary concerts. A full house in the Pavilion Theatre as I appear intermittently to break up the singing with Norfolk-flavoured material. Plenty of chances to underline Cromer-Sheringham rivalry and to poke gentle fun at our visitors seeking temporary refuge in north Norfolk's premier seaside resort. Four local charities drawn out of the hat on stage benefit to the tune of £700 apiece.

Twenty-five years and still singing – providing a few words to go with the songs of the Sheringham Shantymen.

DECEMBER

POOR EXAMPLE (1984) – North-West Norfolk MP Henry Bellingham admits his colleagues don't set much of an example when it comes to addressing letters. During his visit to the Post Office sorting depot in King's Lynn, he sees a pile of 200 letters improperly addressed. And three of them have come from the House of Commons! "It's unbelievable. I'm flabbergasted" says embarrassed Henry.

THANKS A LOT! (1985) – Warmest night of the year. I make my debut as Father Christmas, handing out presents to children with special needs and physical disabilities at the Vauxhall Centre in Norwich. I'm sweltering in that heavy costume and soon learn that eager youngsters bring their own hazards to the party. I threaten to take one lad back to Greenland to help out wrapping presents as he tugs my costume and tries to remove my whiskers. Five minutes later, he returns to tell me his mum says he can go with me. Get out of that one, Santa Skipper!

SMALL PROTEST (1986) – "Christmas" comes out of wraps. I've refused to use the wonderful word on my Radio Norfolk Dinnertime Show until this first day of the month as my small but heartfelt protest against the rising tide of commercialism. The dash to the shops seems to start earlier every year. Many folk agree with my stand, including some traders, but until there's an official embargo I'm afraid the trend is doomed to continue.

NAPPY BONUS (1987) – We get a hint about Yarmouth's priorities ….. Plans to get horses into "nappies" in a bid to clean up the seafront have reined in about £200,000 worth of free publicity for the town, it's claimed at the public services committee. The story of the council's scheme to fit dung-catchers on landau horses reached the national press and prompted letters from overseas. The committee decide to brush aside objections from a local vet and the RSPCA.

TALKING TURKEY (1988) — Bernard Matthews scoffs at a Norwich City Council warning which could turn thousands of families vegetarian this Christmas. He's amazed at a council suggestion that people might like to give turkey the bird and have a non-meat nut roast with their festive trimmings. "I'm surprised they have the temerity to suggest such a thing when they are in the county with Europe's biggest turkey producer employing 2,500 people. I don't think it's patriotic." At the centre of the rumpus is the council's annual campaign to draw attention to salmonella poisoning risks from badly-prepared turkey.

LIGHT PROGRAMME (1989) — Happy family evening at Holt as I help launch the town's Christmas festivities. Slight change to the programme because the sparklers won't light to give the signal for the rocket to be launched to set the church bells pealing to tell the shopkeepers to turn on their lights ... I ask the crowd to join me in an impromptu version of the Norfolk anthem, Hev Yew Gotta Loight, Boy? as launching pad for seasonal activities.

ADVANCED HUMOUR (1990) — I have "retired" from driving after a series of test failures. But I'm geared up for a personal triumph — addressing members of the Institute of Advance Motorists! A bit like asking Bernard Matthews to open a vegetarian restaurant, I suppose, but I am heard with respect. Most of my time is spent lauding our local sense of humour. It must be strong if I can get away with this.

PARISH POWERS (1992) — Parish councils in Norfolk back a move to force district and county councils to consult them on more issues. And they want the more powerful councils to set down their reasons whenever they go against the parish view. They also want a ban on councillors sitting on more than one authority, saying they have fears of divided loyalties under the present system. It all makes good sense — but I doubt if it will come to anything.

TRAM PLANS (1993) — A network of trams could link Norwich with towns throughout Norfolk. A pioneering plan is put forward by the Light Rail Transit Association which would see trams running through the streets and on to rails. This novel transport system, estimated at £200 million pounds, would link Norwich with Yarmouth, Sheringham, Lowestoft and also Dereham and Diss. This is the first time a dual-purpose tram has been considered.

CONSTABLE COUNTRY (1994) — I travel to East Harling with old friend and driving instructor Pat Maitland at the wheel for a WI Victorian Evening. I sing for my supper and then we ask for clear instructions on how to get back on the A11. Suddenly, we are off the beaten track and evidently heading for the beauties of Roudham Heath. We spot lights round a sharp corner and discover a police car. A lone policeman tells us we are indeed going the wrong way and invites us to turn round and follow him back to the land of the living. He asks where we've been in our smart dinner-jackets. We say a WI meeting. He says "Of course, I should have guessed." Then he admits to recognising me and suggests I look better in the paper than I do in the flesh. He points us towards the A11. Yes, a police escort to see us on our way!

MUCKY FATE (1995) — Messy little tale from north Norfolk. A policeman is left feeling very slurry for himself after a cross-country chase. The unnamed officer finds himself waist-deep in pig muck while pursuing an errant moped rider who shows him a clean pair of heels. The incident occurs when police try to stop the moped rider because of a defective rear light. He swerves across the road, abandons his machine and runs into nearby fields followed by the determined officer. The rider scampers up a hill while the policeman takes an alternative route to cut him off — and tumbles straight into some pig slurry.

HOTEL MARDLE (1996) — Intriguing Boxing Day diversion in the shape of a festive mardle to a house party of guests at The Blakeney Hotel. They assemble in the lounge, most of them just returned from an afternoon trip to Norwich Theatre Royal to enjoy the panto, Jack and the Beanstalk. I call my talk Country Christmas, with readings from a variety of books interspersed with personal reflections, light

Allan Smethurst, The Singing Postman — Norfolk's most unlikely pop star.

verses and yarns. The response is cheerful and enthusiastic with several comments about the qualities of Norfolk humour.

GLOWING SPARK (1997) — Jack Spark completes 60 years as clerk to Horsford Parish Council. He has served under nine chairmen, missed just three meetings through illness and may well be the longest-serving parish clerk in Britain. He also carried out a daily milk round on his bike for over half-a-century. He was appointed parish clerk in 1937 for a three-month unpaid trial period. A £10 annual salary followed.

DENNY'S DRIVE (1998) — Tractor driver Denny Thompson calls it a day after 57 years working on the same farm. He followed in his father's tracks in 1941 and went to work at Manor Farm in Guist, not far from Fakenham. There he stays until his boss for 54 of those years, Eric Barratt, sells the farm. "I don't think I would have wanted any other job. I've always been satisfied" says Denny. When he first joined the farm there were 14 workers. He was the only one remaining at the end.

ONE ERA ENDS ... (1999) — Last day of the 1900s. My wife Diane's birthday. Surrounded by family and books, I give thanks for what I have received since being born in dear old Norfolk in 1944 rather than bridle at more recent struggles. It's good to cherish the past but important to embrace the future. I did both recently on going home to open indoor toilets and other facilities in my old village school at Beeston. An icy wind cut across the playground as I shared a few anecdotes and underlined my delight at the school's survival into a fresh century.

LAST POST (2000) — Death at 73 just three days before Christmas of Allan Smethurst, better known as The Singing Postman, Norfolk's most unlikely pop star. He reached the national charts in the 1960s with Hev Yew Gotta Loight, Boy? a song still doing the rounds as the county's unofficial anthem. He was a talented lyricist but hardly cut out to be a performer. He took to drink in a bid to counter stage fright and his time in the spotlight soon ended.

TEAM SPIRIT (2001) — A stirring example of how community spirit can overcome problems. Lotus Cars' director of engineering Simon Wood is driving through the little village of Ketteringham when he hits a patch of ice in his Lotus Elise. He slides off the road and straight into the village hall — all ready for the first Christmas party in the parish. Simon escapes with "bruises and a damaged ego" but the crash leaves the hall unfit for use. Enter Norfolk Fire Service with an offer to host the party in the mess room at their nearby Hethersett headquarters. How to get people there? Now it's the turn of staff at Spratt's Coaches at Wreningham. Mr Wood pays for the coaches.

LOO JACKPOT (2002) — Toilet cleaner Paul Hudson of Aylsham is praised after handing in £900 in a purse he found while working in a loo at Potter Heigham. It belongs to holidaymaker Elsie Jackson, 78, from Barnsley. She sends Paul a letter of thanks and a £50 voucher.

TOP OF TABLE (2004) — Norfolk can boast more village halls and community centres than any other county in England and Wales. The county tops the table of a Charity Commission report which shows its 350 venues had a total annual income of over £3m. However, there's also a warning that such facilities across the country need to keep up to date with trends in society to ensure survival.

CEREAL EVENT (2005) — Locals line up in the porch of their village church to receive sacks of corn, so marking a 250-year-old tradition. Dressed in period costume, bonnets, tunics, tights and black buckled shoes, they gather in the entrance to St Peter's in Strumpshaw. Here they play out a custom that has lasted exactly 250 years, the distribution of wheat by churchwardens to people of the parish.

LABOUR OF LOVE (2006) — Violet Loveday of Attleborough celebrates 80 years as a paid-up member of the Labour Party. She receives a certificate signed by prime minister Tony Blair. Violet joined the party in 1926 at the age of 16. She says she's now a life member after deputy prime minister John Prescott "personally intervened" when she received a recent demand for a £5 membership fee.

*Kathy Staff and a Norfolk "Compo" at the
Theatre Royal, 1982—1983*

NORA BOWS OUT (2008) — Kathy Staff, the actress who played the formidable Nora Batty in television's Last of the Summer Wine, dies at 80. I'm asked by the Eastern Daily Press for a tribute following my appearance as a Norfolk Compo alongside her in the panto *Mother Goose* at Norwich Theatre Royal in 1982-83. She was very helpful on my professional debut, a quiet and thoughtful woman off stage who prayed in her dressing-room before the curtain went up.

GRITTY PAIR (2010) — True grit comes to the streets of Holt as two long-serving councillors take it upon themselves to clear perilous pavements of snow. Holt county councillor John Perry-Warnes says their action is the "shape of things to come", with volunteers likely to have to fill gaps all over Norfolk as public services are scaled back. He's joined by town council chairman Bryan Payne — and the town council's trusty gritting cart.

GIANT PARSNIPS (2011) — A Norfolk farm is forced to sell off tonnes of premium vegetables as animal feed — because a quirk of climate has led to them growing too large to sell to retailers. Giant parsnips are a problem at Tattersett Farms, near Fakenham, which provide root vegetables for a supermarket and have to meet strict size and quality control specifications as part of their contract. Above-average autumn warmth extended the growing season and leads to huge specimens now being harvested.

FINAL NOTES (2012) — A living-room converted into an opera house stages its final shows. The curtain comes down on Claxton Opera at the Old Meeting House in Claxton, near Loddon, after car parking difficulties lead home owner and director Richard White to call it a day after 20 years at the venue. Claxton Opera started 35 years back but after performing in theatres around Norwich, Mr White transformed his home, a converted 18th-century chapel, into an opera house.

WOOLLY BUNCH (2013) — A biblical bunch of woollen characters from the "knitivity" are hidden away in shop windows around Dereham — and the hunt is on to reunite them in time for Christmas Eve. Twelve knitted figures are placed in top-secret town centre locations as part of a competition on behalf of St Nicholas Church. Meanwhile, an auction of celebrities' socks adapted into hand puppets raises £800 for a complex needs school. The online adventure for Sheringham Woodfields School is the idea of youngsters from the Turtle Class.

BIRTHDAY RIDE (2014) — Wymondham butcher Peter Parke thought he'd spend his 80th birthday serving customers at his shop just like he has for almost every day for 60 years. For the man who hasn't taken a holiday since his honeymoon in Clacton in 1957, it might have been a fitting way to mark the milestone. However, keen to tear him away for a few hours, his family organise a surprise open-top bus ride to the Market Cross, where he's met by family, friends and customers.

IT'S BEWTIFUL! (2015) — A real swig of the true Christmas spirit at last in a packed Aylsham parish church. I'm here to share a Norfolk version of the Nativity by Methodist minister Colin Riches. The Aylsham Singers, conducted by Geoff Davidson, provide the musical backcloth for *A Bewtiful Norfolk Christmas*. I insist on that spelling for the programme instead of the Bernard Matthews version of "bootiful."

GOAL RUSH (2015) — It's never the best of omens when your goalkeeper breaks his wrist just before kick-off. But despite having an outfield player between the posts, the setback does little to put Sheringham Reserves off their stride. They trounce Horsford United Reserves 24-0 in the Anglian Combination. Four players complete hat-tricks while Christopher Fuller leads the goal rush with seven.

"The small things in life were often so much bigger than the great things … the trivial pleasure like cooking, one's home, little poems, especially sad ones, solitary walks, funny things seen and overheard"
— Barbara Pym

Lightning Source UK Ltd.
Milton Keynes UK
UKOW05f2251061116
287013UK00007B/20/P